Babes

IN BUSINESS SUITS

Top Women Entrepreneurs
Share Success Secrets

FELICIA PIZZONIA

first edition

THE ULTIMATE PUBLISHING HOUSE (TUPH)
49540 – 80 GLEN SHIELDS AVENUE,
TORONTO, ONTARIO, CANADA, L4K 2B0

Telephone: 647.883.1758 Fax: 416-228-2598
www.tuphpublishing.com
E-mail: admin@tuphpublishing.com
        felicia@feliciapizzonia.com

US OFFICE:
The Ultimate Publishing House (TUPH) P.O. Box 1204
Cypress, Texas, U.S.A. 77410

Ordering Information
Quantity discounts are available on bulk purchases of this book for reselling, educational purposes, subscription incentives, gifts, sponsorship, or fundraising. Unique books or book excerpts can also be fashioned to suit specific needs such as private labelling with your logo on the cover and a message from or a message printed on the second page of the book. For more information please contact our Special Sales Department at The Ultimate Publishing House.

Orders for college textbook / course adoption use.
Please contact the Ultimate Publishing House
Tel: 647 883 1758

TUPH is a registered trademark of The Ultimate Publishing House

PRINTED IN CANADA

Babes In Business Suits, by Felicia Pizzonia
ISBN: 978-0-9819398-2-7
First Edition

Babes
IN
BUSINESS SUITS

Top Women Entrepreneurs
Share Success Secrets

FELICIA PIZZONIA

first edition

Dedications

"I like to live. I like to dance. I like to eat. I like to work and I like my family. I like to enjoy. And ... knock on wood ... it's nice that I can live this way."

— Ivana Trump

For inspiring countless women to achieve their dreams, and for being at the forefront of female entrepreneurialism, this book is respectfully dedicated to Ivana Trump.

Babes in Business Suits proudly showcases the world's top female entrepreneurs, and reveals their secret success strategies for the first time. The Babes share many of the same qualities but are also uniquely different both in background and the various paths they have chose to achieve success, which has motivated me to honor Ivana Trump. Ivana has forged her own path to success all the while retaining those aspects of her personality that are uniquely hers. She has withstood and triumphed, never settling for the expected and is in my mind, the ultimate Babe in a Business Suit.

Ivana is inspirational on so many levels; her triumph over a very public divorce that could have been a disaster, her personal and professional success, and her unfailing grace under pressure has motivated me to dedicate *Babes in Business Suits* to her. Ivana's image evokes class, power, and elegance—all admirable attributes possessed by the Babes who share their stories herein.

True beauty comes from within each of us. A positive attitude, confidence, integrity, honesty, and focus are important attributes demonstrated by Ivana and all of the *Babes in Business Suits,* and qualities that all women can possess.

Ivana, I thank you from the bottom of my heart for your inspiration and for allowing the rest of us to dream your dream, and to achieve success in your wake.

Felicia Pizzonia

Acknowledgments

To my mother, who is the classic female entrepreneur and who has always supported and encouraged me to follow my heart. She is the most incredibly balanced person I know, with perfect harmony of body, mind, and spirit. She has always encouraged me to see the good in all, particularly situations that may seem devastating and to look for the good.

To my family and friends, who have always supported everything I do, and to my mentors, Tasso Lakas, Dini Petty, and T. Harv Eker.

A special thanks to all the women who are part of the book and have partaken in the first of many series of *Babes in Business Suits:* You came into my life exactly at the right moment, and your encouragement, support, and ongoing enthusiasm is the glue that binds this project together.

To all the contributing authors whose life journeys, trials and tribulations, and secrets to success inspired me to help motivate and educate others to live their dreams and passions. We are all part of the universal plan, and all of us—every single one of us—is an important piece of life and the world.

I wish and bless you; all the women of the world, and hope that you live your lives every single day, totally in the moment, focus on the present, and listen to your hearts and the inner voice that tells you what you need to do and why you are here ...you are all stars and it is time to shine!

Table of Contents

Introduction

Introduction

"Success supposes endeavor."
—Jane Austen

In an ever-evolving universe, entrepreneurial initiatives are helping women find greater meaning in their own lives and in the lives of others. We are determined to accomplish our own goals, but we are also committed to helping others succeed and find happiness. For women, success isn't just financial; it is about following our purpose and contributing to the greater good. Now more than ever, we are able to make our own dreams a reality without having to sacrifice nearly as many family priorities as was previously the case, when men worked at the office and women took care of the home. Able to share the time demands associated with raising children and confident enough to find work that inspires us, we are transforming our passions, hobbies, and expertise into successful entrepreneurial ventures.

Babes in Business Suits is a testament to the incredible strength, determination, wisdom, and drive of women. In yesterday's corporate environment, the accomplishments of women were often compared to those of men. This is no longer the case. Women are quickly becoming the barometer for which business success is gauged. As we enter the business world, we carry with us a much-needed sense of balance. By changing the nature of business from primarily profit driven toward stewardship and enrichment, women are encouraging others to do the same. As we open new doors, our diversity and commitment to ourselves and to others helps make the world a better place.

Throughout history, women with courage and fortitude have paved the way for our generation by following their purpose, regardless of the opinions of others. Joan of Arc, Madame Curie, Oprah Winfrey, Louise Hay, Mary Kay, Laura Secord, Michelle Obama, Hillary Clinton, Angelina Jolie and Ivana Trump are just a few who have paved the way and continue to inspire other women to achieve their ultimate dreams and desires.

Unwavering confidence and a strong sense of self empower women to prevail in any entrepreneurial realm. The women in *Babes in Business Suits* are no exception. They have each overcome their own challenges by transforming them into opportunities for personal growth and financial gain. Each woman came from a different background, and continuously strived for the best life possible for them and their family. Let them collectively be a lesson to you that no matter who you are or where you came from, anything is possible and life is limitless. Young and mature women alike have choices and options—we are free to live how we want and set our own rules. *Babes in Business Suits* will help you realize that it is no longer necessary to live according to a predefined role, and that you have the power to define your own life.

In business, the blueprint for success has nothing to do with whether you are a man or a woman. Instead, it is based on characteristics such as integrity, ingenuity, persistence, attitude and vision. Each Babe you meet exhibits each of these traits, and many more. They defined their dreams, followed their passion, and became successes in their own right. The personal struggles and triumphs of each of these women are an invaluable lesson for anyone who wants to forge their own path to success.

The Babes in Business Suits used their innovation to explore new options for their lives and placed no limits on themselves. The only limits we have are self-imposed, and your dedication and willingness to develop your talents and uniqueness is paramount for your success. We were raised to follow in our mothers' footsteps, but many women dared to follow a different path, discovering a real joy in life and never looking back. Women are hurdling obstacles, breaking through boundaries, and saying yes to the life they deserve. When one woman prevails in business, we all advance.

Congratulations! You've just taken the first step toward entrepreneurism. By reading *Babes in Business Suits,* you are embarking on a journey with twelve incredible women who wish you nothing but the best. Inside these pages lies the key to success. It is my sincere wish that you enjoy the knowledge, enthusiasm, and expertise offered by the women you are about to meet in *Babes in Business Suits.*

the Power Within

CHAPTER 1

The Power Within

"I stand for freedom of expression,
doing what you believe in, and going
after your dreams."

— Madonna

We all want some form of success in our lives, but many of us don't know how to achieve it. Worse, many of us don't believe we deserve it. It isn't enough that we empower our physical selves, we also have to empower ourselves mentally. Success involves making a conscious decision that you are worthy, determining what you want, and then taking the necessary steps to achieve your goals. Sounds easy enough, but then how does one explain all the women who stay in dead-end jobs, bad marriages, or just live day-to-day void of any emotion?

Each of us is born with certain abilities and strengths. These vary from person to person, especially in the mental realm, such as math versus language abilities. We also endure certain trials and tribulations, each as unique to us as our own natural capabilities. Now, you may be thinking to yourself, "A good portion of women have experienced divorce, so how is that unique to them?" True, the events themselves are often similar, but the effects of the event are unique. For one woman, a divorce may be a minor inconvenience, but it may turn another woman's world inside out. These reactions are shaped by their beliefs. Far too often, we underestimate the power of our beliefs, but the truth of the matter is that they are the stimulus for the results we receive in life.

Of all the lessons I've ever learned, the most important one is that I need to believe in myself. Our belief in ourselves is the foundation for what we'll accomplish in life. When we talk about our belief systems, the term paradigm is often used. What exactly is a paradigm? According to speaker and author James Arthur Ray, a paradigm is, "The sum total of our beliefs, values, identity, expectations, attitudes, habits, decisions, opinions, and thought patterns—about ourselves, others and how life works…the filter through which we interpret what we see and experience." Our paradigms are the reasons behind our actions. In most cases, paradigms are formed at a very young age and resurface as adult behaviors. Our parents, or any other influential person who had a hand in our childhood, had a certain set of beliefs to which we were exposed. The amount of time you spent with those people determines how much of their belief systems you adopted.

To explain this better, let's take a moment and revisit the two women who went through a divorce: The first, who viewed it as a minor event, may have been brought up in a home where her mother changed husbands like shoes. To the child of this serial divorcee, divorce is just another part of life. The other woman, whose life was shattered due to a divorce, may have grown up in a household where her mother was completely dependent on her father. As a result, this woman's paradigm is that she can't make it on her own and must have a man to support her. This is one of the most common paradigms for women. Women are strong, intelligent, independent, and fully capable of becoming successes in their own right, but when negative or traumatic events happen to us, we sometimes feel that life is too difficult and a sense of powerlessness sets in.

Relinquishing Your Past

CAN WE DEVELOP a new set of beliefs? Is it possible for us to believe that we have untapped reservoirs of power capable and that we are capable of creating the lives we desire? The answer is unquestionably yes! But to rid ourselves of our paradigms or limiting beliefs, we need to determine their source. Only then can we replace these false beliefs with realistic and encouraging ones. I like to refer to this as checking your baggage. We need to gather up all our old belief systems that no longer serve us, place them in a suitcase with no address label, zip it up, drive to the airport, and check the bag on a one-way flight to nowhere. This is the only way to become empowered and to go after the life we dream of and deserve.

Before we can head to the airport, we need to discover the origins of our paradigms. To do this, we must reflect on our lives and remember any significant events, circumstances, and experiences. Did something happen in the past to affect your self-esteem or self-image? When you think of money, success, or empowerment, are you bombarded with negative thoughts? If you are, then ask yourself, "What is blocking my ability to transform my life for the better?" Just as an orange construction sign blocks the entrance to a construction site, limiting beliefs prevent you from entering the life of your dreams. To remove the block, you need to understand a little bit of how your mind works.

The mind is an amazing machine. Notice that I didn't say organ here, because although your brain is an organ, your mind is something entirely different. Our minds have two distinct sections—the conscious and the subconscious. The conscious mind is where all of your sensory input is gathered, while the subconscious mind is your "feeling" mind, which stores all of your memories (even those you are not aware of on a conscious level).

Limiting beliefs are stored in the subconscious mind, so we need to dig deep and bring the lies we've been telling ourselves to the surface. Most of our minds have been programmed or repeatedly subjected to certain messages. It's actually quite similar to computer programming; only the type of data is different. Instead of binary codes and calculations, our minds are programmed with both positive and negative emotions when we are young. Unfortunately, the negative emotions have far more devastating effects and can include things such as self-doubt, fear, anxiety, and insecurity, just to name a few. So essentially, our paradigms are programmed limitations turned into reality. The good news is that, just like any software, these programs can be deleted.

Once we acknowledge these sabotaging thoughts, our minds are limitless and so is our potential. This is the moment we experience true personal empowerment, realizing that we can handle everything in life. We need to shift our thinking and realize that thoughts become things. It's crucial that we act in the present moment, the way things are, not how they were in the past. For example, as a publisher, I expect that The Ultimate Publishing House will publish several hundred authors' books each year. I expect it, I feel it, I see it. I am a visionary and I take action, and this is the perfect recipe for anything you want to achieve. Being a visionary is very important; you have to see everything you want to happen, from start to finish. It is important that we make a conscious choice to replace our limiting beliefs with ones that propel us forward.

What Do You See in The Mirror?

WHEN YOU LOOK in the mirror, what do you see? Fear, doubt, anxiety, and maybe even hate? Or do you see a confident woman ready to take on the world? Your self-esteem is nothing more than how you feel about yourself—either you like yourself or you don't. If I were to ask you to list ten of your talents off the top of your head, could you do it? How about five, or even just three? Most individuals with low self-esteem have a hard time identifying their abilities because they simply don't believe they have anything of value to offer the world.

Low self-esteem causes depression, insecurity, and a lack of fulfillment. The constant stream of negative self-talk that often results from low self-esteem impacts our ability to face our fears and ultimately to build our confidence. We lose that "I can do anything" attitude. One of the best gifts that you can give yourself is healthy self-esteem. We need to feel accepted by others and to be valued for what we do and who we are, and building self-esteem is a vital step toward fulfillment in life. You must love yourself first, and then others will follow.

People can be mean and nasty, and as much as we'd sometimes like to, we can't rely on others to validate our worth. Women with poor self-esteem are not only subjected to their own paradigms, but to other people's perceptions as well. Without healthy self-esteem, self-sabotaging thoughts can easily infiltrate your life and cause you to wonder constantly about what others think of you. Consequently, you lose confidence in yourself—if you had any to begin with—and feel powerless over your life. What other people think about you, is none of your business!

Do you draw your self-esteem from external sources that may cause you to crumble when they fail? Where do you get your self-worth? Does your value derive from others or from yourself? Do you evaluate your life based on the opinions of others? If someone drives a Mercedes while you're driving a Kia, do you feel less valuable than that person? What about your weight? Do you sometimes want to stay home because you don't like the way you look? Why? Good things come in packages of all shapes and sizes. You make your results, not your weight, your money, or your car. It's tempting to constantly compare yourself to others, but it can quickly become all-consuming. If it's not one thing, it's another, and before you know it nothing in your life is as good as your neighbor's, co-worker's, friend's, family's, or the stranger's walking down the street. In the end, you just feel inadequate. No matter who you are, someone is going to be thinner, prettier, or have more money, so stop measuring yourself and your life against other people and what they have. The universe gives us what we need, and when you're ready, it will give you unlimited gifts. The universe always has your back, remember that, TRUST and expect only the BEST!

We are responsible for our own self-esteem and confidence. By respecting ourselves, we can improve our relationships with others, our careers, and our lives. To improve your self-esteem, focus on your good qualities. You might not believe in them yet, but they are there. Remember those paradigms; they're persistent and will find any means possible to creep back into your mind. As I do with The Ultimate Publishing House, visualize your success, and make the vision as specific as possible. Avoid making generic goals; knowing exactly what you want will make it that much easier to achieve. It's imperative that you believe in the value and gifts you have to offer the world. Once you develop a healthy opinion of yourself, you will have a sense of personal empowerment. Finally, keep in mind that you, and only you, can determine your self-worth; no one else can have any power over you and your emotions unless you allow it!

Seeing is Believing

DECIDE WHAT YOU want most out of life. Ask yourself, *"What do I want to become?"* Now visualize yourself accomplishing your desire. As you visualize your ideal person, feel the empowerment flow through and around you. Remember, even if you don't believe it yet, you are strong, self-confident, and in charge of your own destiny.

Visualization involves developing an image and holding it in your mind's eye as a permanent record that can be recalled at any time. When I visualize something, I do so in the form of a movie. For example, I watch The Ultimate Publishing House publish one hundred books per year with authors in every country playing on the screen in my mind. I don't visualize this happening in the future—visualizations must be in the now. If you want to become CEO of a multi-million dollar corporation, you can't visualize yourself in that position when you lose ten pounds, or after your children have left for college. You have to see it happening in the present tense. Besides, most multi-million dollar corporations have in-house daycare facilities and fitness centers.

Be aware that this works both ways. If you envision yourself as someone who is unsuccessful or unhappy, you will get those results. To visualize successfully, you need to eliminate all negative thoughts and focus only on the positives, capturing all your healthy desires and shutting out any negative images. Negative thoughts that creep in weaken your visualization bit by bit and render it powerless.

Visualization builds self-belief. When you visualize yourself as that CEO, you are building a picture of yourself as a successful businesswoman. This contributes to your positive self-belief and enables you to reject any self-doubt and sabotaging thoughts. The key to successful visualization is consistency. You can't develop an image for one day and expect to wake up the next morning to find it has come to fruition. The more frequently you visualize, the stronger your self-belief becomes, increasing your chances of accomplishing your goal. Visualization builds self-esteem because it replaces self-doubt with a positive perception of yourself and your abilities.

Combining your visualizations with positive affirmations increases your ability to channel your focus and eliminate the many negative distractions we face in life. This process helps to keep you focused and productive. It is just as important to use the present tense with affirmations as it is with visualizations. For instance, make statements such as, "I am…," rather than, "I will be…." This makes your affirmations much more effective, and amplifies your results. Keep in mind that, just like visualizations, affirmations can work for or against you, so be conscious of your words. An example of an affirmation would be; I am so happy and excited now that I sold 2 homes or more in August 2009!

Affirmations also help improve your self-esteem and confidence. Think about how good you feel when someone compliments you—one kind word can turn your whole day around. Now imagine what a steady stream of positive affirmations will do for your self-esteem. Once you learn how to use visualizations and affirmations together effectively, your self-worth and confidence will go through the roof. Before you know it, you'll be empowered to take on the world.

Live Inwardly and Outwardly

SELF-EMPOWERMENT HELPS you connect to your true self and learn what fuels you and also what drains your creative energy. This knowledge will enable you to manage and master your fate. As women, we must believe that true empowerment is not only psychological, but also spiritual. With all of the negativity in the media today, the competition in the workplace, and the overall gloom and doom surrounding us, we must find a way to bring positive energy into our lives. Let go of the pettiness and needless worry in your life, and shift your focus to one of healing and gratitude. Set an example for those around you by acting in a peaceful, positive manner. Once you've made this shift, you are on the path to spiritual empowerment.

Once we eliminate the emotional clutter and distraction from our lives we can clarify who we are and what we believe. With spiritual empowerment, we gain the ability to listen to ourselves and tune into our intuition. It is intuition that tells us the person we want to be and allows us to become our true selves. All the answers you need are within you, simply quiet the mind, don't; think for a few seconds or better yet minutes. This reduces our stress and strengthens our inner being, leading us to live in harmony with the universe's energy, inwardly and outwardly balanced. Once we understand how this balance of energy empowers us, we can learn to harness this energy and truly live our best lives.

Psychological and spiritual empowerment puts you in control of your life as you gain strength and understand what your goals are. Although there are rules to follow, you understand that we only get one chance at life and every day that we don't live our true empowered life is a day we will never get back. You must make decisions that will be in your own best interest and in harmony with who you are as a person. When you realize that you can be decisive and use good judgment, you give yourself the empowerment that you need to be successful.

Empowerment gives you the ambition and drive you need to lose weight, get a better job, become a *Babe in a Business Suit,* or just be happier. You can break barriers, create new goals, and look at life with a new set of eyes. Empowerment frees you from limitations and enables you to take full responsibility for everything in your life. It's about being in control.

Take time in life to ensure that your actions really mean something. You need to create inspirational goals for yourself and make sure that you are taking steps to make them happen. One of the most important lessons I want to share is this: It doesn't matter if you succeed or fail, all that matters is that you know what empowerment feels like. Trust me, once you have this feeling, you will never want to let it go. Once you achieve empowerment, successes soon outweigh failures and your life will evolve into the one you've always imagined. You can choose success or you can choose to sit on the couch and watch soap operas. The decision is yours. Remember, what you think, is what will happen!

Empowerment equals choices. Only you have the right to choose the life you want, and you deserve to live a full and confident life. Stop beating yourself up with those useless old paradigms and limiting beliefs. The past is gone and cannot be altered, so focus on today and look forward to the future but always be present, since this moment is what you have, forget about the past and the future, the present is a gift and enjoy it! Ask yourself, "What choices do I have to empower myself today?" Take responsibility for your actions, stop making excuses, replace destructive beliefs with encouraging ones, and you will take back control of your life. Let me leave you with a final thought: Silver tarnishes and diamonds start out as coal, but you wouldn't know this just by looking at them in a jewelry store. There is beauty in everything and though we may sometimes lose our luster, we are still powerful, strong, and intelligent women. As long as you believe in yourself, anything is possible.

Attitude

CHAPTER 2

Attitude

"Happiness is an attitude.
We either make ourselves miserable,
or happy and strong. The amount
of work is the same."
— **Francesca Reigler**

What is attitude? Viktor Frankl wrote: "Everything can be taken away from a person but one thing, the last of human freedoms, to choose one's attitudes in any set of given circumstances, to choose one's own way." Indeed, there is only one aspect of your life that you always have complete control over, and that is your attitude. This is the most powerful word in life. Responding to a negative situation and remaining objective, rather than reacting to it, is the winner's choice. There are so many things wrong in the world, but you must choose not to allow them to affect you and to focus on what is good and positive. It takes work to train yourself to focus on the good, but with practice you can learn to set aside old thoughts about lack and limitation. This allows you to see beauty in the most mundane and everyday occurrence and live in a state of gratitude and awe.

As Earl Nightingale once said, *"A great attitude does much more than turn on the lights in our worlds; it seems to magically connect us to all sorts of serendipitous opportunities that were somehow absent before the change."* Enthusiasm for your future, and the possibilities it holds, is the natural extension of a positive attitude. It is important to feel, love, and believe that you can achieve anything, because you can! Thoughts become things. The thoughts you focus on will manifest themselves in your life and come to pass, and it takes just as much energy to think small as it does to think big. So, aim for the moon and reach for the stars.

As a child, you had a great imagination. You may have even had an invisible friend or a pet. Over the years, however, your imagination likely faded, and your attitude and level of enthusiasm may have shifted as well. You need to put your attitude back on the top of your list and use it as your number one source for ideas and dreams. Go back to being three years old. You were fully open to receive and were happy for no apparent reason, you were simply living in bliss because life is beautiful. The secret ingredient in any recipe for success is attitude. When you wake up every morning, your first thought should be one of appreciation. In fact, speak aloud and say all the things you are grateful for in your life. The first thing I do every morning is open my eyes and thank God for everything, particularly my healthy body, the roof over my head, my family and friends, and the opportunity to be alive. Then I ask myself, "How can I serve today and add value to people's lives?"

The key to life is living in the present moment. Be happy and grateful for today, because you never know if tomorrow will come. In the spirit of living in the moment, let's take action right now. Put this book aside for a moment and write a list of what and whom you are grateful for. Read the list aloud and really feel it. When you think of something very intently until you begin to really feel it, your thoughts and feelings align in something that is called vibrational integrity. This is the ultimate form of manifestation, and it puts your wishes out into the universe so you attract who and what you need to fulfill your life goals. The universe always has your back.

I love Albert Einstein. He once said that you must attach yourself to a worthy cause, not to people or things, and I couldn't agree more. We are all part of a big plan, and we all have a purpose. It is our duty to have a positive attitude, be aware of what we have to do, and to do it with passion and grace. Life is a beautiful adventure and we are meant to experience it with pleasure and to enjoy the journey. Our goals are important, and we will reach them all with diligence, perseverance, and a positive attitude, but we must remember to enjoy the journey. Whenever you feel frustrated or discouraged, please remember the words, "this too shall pass," because it will. Try to have fun, and don't take life too seriously or it may simply pass you by. Life is a beautiful adventure—never forget that, and you will live life to the fullest!

My passions are marketing and book publishing. I love what I do and do it whole-heartedly. I always tell people to think about this: If you had one hundred million dollars in your bank account, what would you do for a living? If you choose your current job or career, you are on the right life path! If your answer is something other than what you are doing, then you need to think about what makes you happy and what do you need to do to get on that track. My answer was that I would be publishing books for entrepreneurial authors and youth and teen authors. With my publishing house, The Ultimate Publishing House, this is exactly what I am doing.

The Secret to Attitude and Sales

BEFORE LAUNCHING The Ultimate Publishing House, I worked with Bob Proctor, who, among his many accolades, was featured in the hit movie, The Secret. While working with Bob, I hit record sales numbers and earned the title Super Salesman. One day, he asked me my secret to closing deals. He was particularly curious because I rarely left my office and had the ability to sell publishing deals without getting out of my seat. I told Bob that my secret was that I didn't think of it as "closing," because that word has negative connotations—who wants to be closed? I don't.

I believe that, in life and in business, people want a relationship and to know that they are important. So each morning, I wake up and think, "How can I add value, and how may I serve?" When I go on a sales call, I'm thinking, "I have $100 million in my bank account, I do what I do because I love it. The purpose of the call is to add value, and help." I don't go in for the "close," I go in with the invitation to join, and it works every time! If you carry out your actions with pure intent, the money will follow. It certainly worked for me—applying this premise helped me sell millions of dollars in goods and services over the past decade. Consider this: we spend more of our time working than we do at leisure, so shouldn't we be doing the things that we love?

Paradigms

PARADIGMS CONVINCE US we are limited to certain actions, and it can be very difficult to move past that thought pattern once it's firmly established. Paradigms could be controlling virtually every move you make. Once you understand how to build a positive paradigm to replace the one that presently controls your life, you will have opened a door to a brand new world. At birth, your mind is wide open, but over the years, we inherit our parent's ideals, opinions, thoughts, and ethics, as well as those of the media, school, society and everything around us. Think about it! I'm willing to bet that one of your paradigms involves money. Do any of the following statements sound familiar?

- *Money doesn't grow on trees.*

- *To be financially secure, you need to get an education, find a good job, stay put, and retire at 65.*

- *Money is evil.*

- *I don't have enough money, or enough time.*

In the space below, list some paradigms that may be holding you back from your greatness.

1. _____

2. _____

3. _____

4. _____

5. _____

6. _____

7. _____

8. _____

9. _____

10. _____

NOW, GO BACK And review your list. How many of these are false and originated from outside sources? Do these beliefs truly reflect who you are? Let's take a moment and revisit the money paradigm. Instead of thinking about how much money you don't have, why not focus on the money you do have? For example, change your thought process to "Money comes easy to me. I love what I do, so I am not working, I am playing. I add value to people's lives and businesses, so I reap the rewards."

Now, in the space below, write a list of your true beliefs, as if you were born again with a clear slate.

My true beliefs are:

1. *Money is a GOOD motivator and tool that helps me create and exchange energy.*

2. _____

3. _____

4. _____

5. _____

6. _____

7. _____

My true beliefs are:

8. _____

9. _____

10. _____

AS ENTREPRENEURS, WE aren't just business people—we are problem solvers. We find solutions that better our own lives as well as those of other people, and a positive attitude allows us to see these opportunities. Earl Nightingale is best known as a motivational writer and author. He believes that "Whatever we plant in our subconscious mind and nourish with repetition and emotion will one day become a reality." Always maintain that happy attitude—visualize yourself holding a beautiful, fragrant bouquet, and go through your day with that image in your mind. Always remember that our attitude towards others determines their attitude towards us so our treatment of others will determine our experience each day.

Our environment the world in which we live and work, is a mirror of our attitudes and expectations. A great attitude does much more than open the door to possibility; it connects us to a wide variety of serendipitous opportunities that were noticeably absent prior to our change in perspective. The mind moves in the direction of our current dominant thoughts, so what's going on inside our mind manifests itself on the outside. We can let circumstances and events rule us or we can take charge and rule our lives from within. Whether they want to admit it or not, people are where they are in life because that's exactly where they really want to be. We all walk in the dark at times, and each of us must learn to turn on our light. Whenever we're afraid, it's because we are facing the unknown. Once we understand that fear is an emotion and we have control over our emotions, we can choose to set aside that fear and still achieve whatever goals we set.

Neale Diamond Walsh once said, "The person standing on the mountaintop did not get there by falling." You have to climb to where you want to be, and you can't get there by climbing over others. It is about climbing with others, side by side, and sometimes even pulling others up with you. Are you willing to do that? If you are, you'll get to your destination, and importantly, others will be happy you're there. In order to scale your own heights, evaluating your progress each and every day is important and this doesn't require a long intense program or process. You can start very simply, at the end of each day.

David Freemantle, author of *The Buzz*, a book on improving customer service, offers these end-of-day review practices, which can be applied to personal development in your own life. Every evening, sit down, read the bullet points below, review your attitude, and vow to wake up the next morning with a more positive outlook than the day before.

- At the end of every day, spend five minutes with your family or friends and share stories about the positive events that happened that day.

- Sit quietly for five minutes or so every evening to reflect on the positive choices you make at work and at home that day. Write these down and remind yourself of them the next day.

- Be curious about things you don't know and don't understand. Perhaps try something new each day to expand the world you live in and continue to reach for a more fulfilling life.

You as a Brand

CHAPTER 3

You as a Brand

"If I lost control of the business I'd lose myself—or at least the ability to be myself. Owning myself is a way to be myself."

— Oprah Winfrey

What comes to mind when you think of a pair of golden arches, hear the phrase, "I'd like to teach the world to sing," or see the image of a bitten apple? Unless you've been living in a cave for the past several decades, you think of Starbucks, Coca-Cola, and Apple computers. Silhouette-shaped bottles with red cursive lettering, and little white apples all represent internationally known brands. Today's businesses all share at least one common marketing practice: a strong and positive brand image.

Branding isn't just for products, services, and companies any more. It is also for you. Branding is essential because it defines who you are, what you stand for, and what makes you unique. I can't think of a successful company that doesn't have a strong, easily recognizable brand—probably because no such company exists! So how do you go about creating a brand? First, you need to register your name as a domain name. Visit Godaddy.com, a popular website that allows you to do this for just ten dollars. Trust me—this is one of the best investments you'll ever make. Then create your own personal email address. For example, if your name is Mary Jacobs, your e-mail address could be mary@maryjacobs.com.

Think for a moment about the importance of your own domain name and e-mail address. If a potential client wants to contact you but doesn't have your information, all they have to do is Google your name and they can find your website and contact information within seconds. People want fast results and won't take the time to sort through a pile of business cards or search for your name in the (antiquated) phone book, so be sure to create a presence on the internet.

Branding is the foundation of marketing and is inseparable from business strategy. It is more than putting a label on a fancy product—your brand is a combination of you and your company's unique attributes, communicated through a name or symbol that influences a thought process in the mind of an audience. In other words, branding establishes a reputation with consumers. Personal branding is the key to success. People want to do business with people they know or with whom they feel some sort of connection. If you have a familiar and consistent presence, people will feel like they know you and will be more receptive to doing business with you. In the competitive business world, you have to brand yourself to distinguish yourself and your services and products from everyone else.

If we are going to have a business, we need to have a strong image associated with it. Business stationery, logos, and a website are no longer enough. Branding isn't just about business cards and letterhead, it's also about building relationships with clients. How you interact with clients, what you say to them, and how they perceive you is your brand. Branding is about showing people, not just telling them, who you are and what you do.

Creating a unique brand is the best way to gain name recognition and generate sales and profits. A brand helps your clients remember you and all that you have to offer. Studies have shown that it costs five times more to gain a customer than it does to retain one. Today, so many companies are competing for the same dollar that people need an image to remind them who you are and what your service or product is about. A strong brand sticks in the minds of potential clients or customers and gives you the power to promote your business. By creating a unique and lasting brand, your product or service sells itself.

When you create a strong brand, your trademark attracts people to your business. Your brand gives you the freedom to express not only what you sell, but also who you are as a person. In the last chapter, we talked about integrity and how many choose integrity over products or services. In this sense, your brand is your résumé. It gives any potential client a quick overview of who you are and what you're all about, so your brand's image should reflect your core values.

A brand is much more than just promoting and marketing yourself to others. In DotZen, Dr. Seamus Phan says, "...the core of branding, beyond telling truth, is to be true to yourself." In this spirit, the first thing you need to do is look deeply inside yourself and at your business and ask these questions: "Why am I creating this business?" "How will others see me?" "How do I see myself?"

Your brand must be consistent with your purpose. Your purpose will evolve over time, so be careful in the initial stages of deciding on a brand, and take the time to think about how your business might change or grow in the future. Will your brand still reflect who you are in twenty years? Keep in mind that you have to evolve with your brand, not the other way around People change; brands don't. Once the public defines an image and sets it in their minds, it is there forever. Starbucks has positioned itself as the neighborhood coffee shop so much that it has completely infiltrated our everyday lives. Now every time someone even says the word "latte" an image of the Starbuck's logo appears in your head. This is the strength of connection that a strong brand image conveys. The correct brand image allows you to communicate your message in a clear, concise, and precise manner.

Madonna is one of the best examples of brand identity. Would you consider her to be the same person she was a couple of decades ago, rolling around on stage wearing skimpy clothes? Clearly this isn't the case she is now a mother, a humanitarian, and an accomplished singer and actor. She has changed over the years, but her basic brand of sexuality and taboo envelope pushing has never changed. She is and always will be an independent, sexy, in-your-face superstar. When we see Madonna, she delivers what we expect of her, but imagine how her audiences would react if she walked out on stage wearing a prairie dress with her hair in a bun. They would feel cheated, because she wouldn't be staying true to her branding.

Let the world know what is so special about you and why your services or products are what they need. Let your brand speak for you and sing your praises.

Three fundamental principles define a good branding image:

- **Consistency:** Your brand is the basis for your business and for how you are viewed by others, so your actions should be consistent with your brand's message. Consistency is the key that can unlock the door to success. If you consistently position your product or company in the way you want it to be perceived by comsumers, you will be successful. There is no alternative.

- **Authenticity:** Your brand should be intimately connected to your soul and desires, creating a true reflection of you and your business. Ask yourself if this brand truly represents who you are and the goals you want to achieve.

- **Clarity:** A distinct, clear message with no conflicting values lets your customers know exactly where you stand and how you operate in all of your professional endeavors.

When you align your brand with these three important principles, you send a clear message that people recognize and trust.

First Impressions

WE ALL KNOW how important first impressions are, in business and in life. This applies to branding as much as anything else. A person's first impression of your brand determines how the rest of your business relationship will unfold. If your brand conveys the right message, it can be very successful. Within minutes of seeing your brand, a potential customer can decide if you will be competent, honest, valuable, or beneficial to them. First impressions last, whether positive or negative. Making a good first impression is important, especially if the people you meet can affect the direction of your business.

Typically, first impressions are made the first time you meet a person. However, sometimes you make an impression even before you meet a person, which is the case with your brand. In the past, a person had to walk into your business to meet you and learn about your brand, but this is no longer the case. Businesses now have their own websites, e-mail, blogs, and webinars. Your choice of words, greetings, and manner of speaking gives the customer a glimpse of what kind of person you are and how you run your business. Unprofessional and poorly designed website content tells potential customers a lot about your brand, so it is vital that every aspect of your branding be well executed and truly reflect the image you wish to portray.

It is also important to realize that potential clients will likely do some research before completing any transactions with you. Whenever you put information about yourself in front of an audience, whether on a website or blog, ensure that it is professional and representative of who you want to be. Making a lasting positive first impression on people can be very beneficial in the long run, and businesses and brands that make a good first impression are guaranteed to see a positive return from their clients.

Credibility

IN ANY KIND of entrepreneurial endeavor, credibility is vital. This is particularly the case for women. As we forge our own path in the business world, we need to make sure that we do so with integrity and a credible message. Building credibility should be one of the main objectives in operating a business, because your business can't grow and expand if your customers don't trust you, and without customers, you don't have a business.

Building your identity is important to building a strong customer relationship. Your brand is an excellent tool for letting people know who you are, so make it a priority to create a brand that conveys a message of trustworthiness and credibility. It may not seem that important to some, but historically, the most successful businesses have been accompanied by a positive brand.

Take a moment and imagine that you are looking for a company to produce a book for you. Now, let's assume that you have the contact information of two businesses offering the same packages. One has a brand backed with a credible message that conveys their desire to serve you and help you succeed. The other provides nothing other than a name and phone number. Which one would you choose?

Most would choose the one with the positive brand identity because it builds an immediate sense of trust and credibility. People want to do business with companies that are just as interested in their success as they are. When your brand makes you look professional and credible to your customers, you'll not only generate success but also create lasting relationships.

Every day, we are bombarded with commercials for companies and their services. They all have the goal of attracting or retain you as their customer, but the deciding factor is an effective brand. When people trust your brand

and associate you with a positive experience, success is inevitable. To succeed, any business must have credibility, which is why they have to pull out all the stops to make sure customers recognize them in a positive light. Using your brand is the best and most effective way to achieve this reaction.

Once, it was all about location, location, location; now it is all about branding yourself. You don't just want your business to stand out, you want it to stand above the rest. No one wants to be thought of as merely "that business," at least not if they are serious about succeeding. A brand cements a concrete image in the world's mind about who you are and what you do.

Personal branding is more than just searching through a thesaurus, giving your business a catchy name, and placing an ad on the radio and in the newspaper. Your brand is more than just words; it is you. Brand yourself before others do it for you. It is imperative that we have control over our image and the perceptions and ideas that other people have about us.

In a world where advertising is everywhere, branding positions you and your company firmly in the minds of existing and potential customers. Having a strong, recognizable, and memorable brand means that you don't have to waste money on unnecessary advertising to compete for business. You've established a relationship through your brand, so customers already know you.

Ideally, you want your brand to become so ingrained in your customers' minds that they are reminded of it several times throughout the day. When they drive to work, they see a billboard and instantly think of you. When they listen to the radio, they hear a song and think of you. This symbolic identification can reap massive rewards. Keep your customers and the nature of your business in mind as you create your company's trademark or logo. Something as simple as a font, for example, can be hip, conservative, classic, clean, contemporary, busy, elegant, edgy, and so on. Whatever you choose, it should be a positive and recognizable symbol of your product or service. The

Nike swoosh epitomizes this idea. People no longer need to see the brand name to recognize the company; when they see the symbol, they know it's Nike. What message do you want to express with your logo?

I've included a few important branding tips to help you with the process:

- Design a logo that looks good in black and white, printed, on letterhead, billboards, websites, advertisements, or vehicles.

- Be original. Your brand should make the public think of you and only you. Don't copy someone else, because when clients see your brand, they are also seeing your competitor's. Step as far outside of the box as possible when designing your brand.

- Simple is best. Studies have shown that a simple logo is more recognizable and identifiable to customers than one with many elements. Again, think of the Nike swoosh. Pure genius!

- Use vector graphics that can be resized without distortion.

- Protect your logo via patent or registered trademark. Consult the U.S. Patent Office at www.uspto.gov.

SUCCESSFUL BRANDING COMES from within—who you are today as well as the dreams of who you want to be. You can live your dreams if you put in the effort. Present your clients with the same image every time they turn to your business and without fail, you'll elevate yourself above the competition.

Babe in Tweed

CHAPTER 4

Jeri Walz:
Babe in Tweed

"Who we are in our truth is perfect, whole, and complete, right here and right now. Everything that we need to create our successes, joy, and happiness is already within, not without."

— Jeri Walz

I grew up in San Diego, California, the youngest of four children, with two sisters and a brother. My father, who meant everything to me, died in a plane crash when I was twelve and my mother struggled with her alcoholic demons. I spent most of my teenage years feeling absolutely alone, often driving up to the Cuyamaca Mountains to a favorite rock that overlooked a magnificent, flowing valley. I would sit there and sort out my life, beginning to dream about how things would turn out. It was there that I found myself connected to my truth, and I returned, more than forty years later, to the very rock where my spiritual journey began.

As I sat overlooking the valley, I found myself in a state of melancholy, missing my early years of wonderment. At first, this mood puzzled me, until I remembered that the present moment includes all that is and all that was in my journey. Reflecting with gratitude for my life's journey, my mood shifted to complete joy and happiness. I recognized the undeniable truth that I had realized all the success, dreams, and happiness that I had envisioned for myself back then on this same sacred spot.

My early dreams centered on being in a lifelong loving relationship where my partner and I were mutually supportive of each other's dreams and aspirations. At that time, it was hard to believe that this was possible because I had no reference point among the people I knew. Since I was going to have to start from scratch on my dreams, I wrote a list of my dreams in my journal. They included having a family, being professionally and financially accomplished, having true friendships, loving animals, and making a difference in my life and in the lives of the people who cross my path.

Life has a wonderful way of leveling the playing field of your dreams when it presents itself in all its cold reality. In the search to realize my financial dreams I experienced, more than once, the pain and anguish of not knowing where my next dollar would come from or how I was going to pay my bills. I discovered that the thinking surrounding money, or the lack thereof, was a spiritual lesson, and that the amount of money I earned was in direct proportion to my consciousness about money.

Harnessing Fear

THERE IS AN old saying, "Ride a horse in the direction it is going." I noticed early on that fear seemed to be pretty constant in my life, so I decided to embrace it and welcome its presence. I discovered that fear has different faces. There is the obvious fear of death when danger appears; however, there is another fear that shows up when entering new levels of spiritual and emotional growth. I learned to welcome fear as a sign that I was growing. This was never clearer than when I found myself working a series of dead-end jobs in my twenties. After several failed attempts at success in the business world, I finally decided to listen to my mother and get my real estate license. This required me to change my view of my abilities, and fear cropped up. Knowing that welcoming fear made all the difference in the world, I started in real estate in 1974, when the real estate market was one of the worst in history. There was a lot of limited thinking about the market, but with my intuitive knowledge that success comes from within, I set out on what would become a wonderful and successful journey. On this journey, I discovered quite a bit about myself and what I was made of. My most significant discovery was that I am the business. I soon grasped the idea that my fear was an acknowledgement of my growth into uncharted waters and I embraced it. From then on, each time fear showed up, I reminded myself to focus on where I was going and what I really wanted.

Thinking and Vision

IT WAS DURING these early years in real estate that my primary consciousness breakthroughs occurred, especially about money. Creating my vision for success has been central to my achievements. I discovered through the study of metaphysics that what we think manifests itself in our physical universe and that vision trumps limited thinking. Accordingly, I regularly upgraded my vision for my success. As a result, I became an expert at selling new projects for builders. Some of the largest builders in southern California contracted with me to sell their projects, and I successfully sold thousands of new homes. I discovered time and time again that the way I think is the cause of my success, and that my power as a successful businesswoman is grounded in the belief that we all have a God-given ability to use thought and vision to develop our individual skills.

Recognizing that we always have a choice when it comes to our attitude has been another key to my success, along with embracing the belief that I am co-creator and I attract exactly what I need for my lessons on this planet. This earthly experience is my opportunity for internal growth and to learn to accept love and joy into my life and share it with others. Many people find it difficult to make the connection between spiritual thought and financial success because of a perceived conflict between spiritual and financial beliefs. However, my professional journey is a testament to the fundamental connection between the two.

Here I am, more than forty years later, on the rock overlooking the valley, reflecting on my life's journey. This journey has included marrying Rod, my best friend; raising four self-actualized children; having wonderful, loving animals and great friends; and achieving significant financial success. I reflected on how I transformed my thinking to believe that life happens for you, not to you.

After a successful fourteen-year career in the real estate brokerage business and meeting my husband, Rod, we risked everything we owned and founded Walz Certified Mail Solutions (Walz Group). Rod and I had a vision of transforming the way companies executed critical mailings using the United States Postal Service's Certified Mail. In fact, we even had to change the thinking and mindset of the USPS, a formidable challenge. After growing through the difficult early years, we expanded our product and service vision, and brought in complementary partners as a measurement of our expanded financial consciousness. In 2008, *INC. 500 Magazine* named Walz the 45th fastest growing company in the United States, and 4th fastest growing service company. Today, my husband and I have both stepped away from the day-to-day operations of our company and it continues to grow and prosper on the same spiritual and financial principles upon which it was founded. It is rewarding to know that our company has saved other companies and government agencies millions of dollars over the years, and provided a great opportunity for our employees to grow both personally and professionally in a forward-thinking atmosphere at a time when the general economy is suffering.

As we navigated through the challenges of growing Walz Certified Mail Solutions to its ultimate success, we remained true to our principles of thought and vision, and, together with welcoming fear, this proved to be the biggest key to our success. Nevertheless, I continue to see people whose business plans do not incorporate these principles, and who don't appreciate fear as a bellwether

Babe in Tweed

47

of their growth, and have thus allowed it to be a personal and professional barrier. People often say that you need to overcome your fear, but this type of thinking assumes that fear is a negative. It is my experience that understanding and welcoming fear is a fundamental key to success.

Focus and Manifestation

ANOTHER PRINCIPLE OF success that I discovered is that when we focus on things, they manifest themselves. I was in a restaurant recently, and as a waiter was heading to the kitchen with a handful of dishes, a patron yelled out, "Don't drop it!" Well, guess what? The waiter's mind focused on dropping the dishes, and the crash resounded throughout the restaurant. Our minds don't just listen to the thoughts of others, but to our own as well, both positive and limiting. It was essential to my successes that I took great care to focus on the right things. For example, when fear came up, rather than focus on the fear, I focused on my vision. Vision is something beyond what we already know, and though the unknown confronts us with fear, that is where the most growth is possible.

When we focus on our vision and welcome the fear, we operate at a higher level, so we must focus on our vision and accept everything that happens as a perfect step on the way to that vision. We become whatever we allow ourselves to dwell upon mentally. My success with the Walz Group is just a matter of my willingness to welcome my fears and take action, regardless of the circumstances. We all need to welcome fear in order to start really living the life we want to live—the life we deserve. I got where I am by never giving up and embracing my fears.

Trust Your Vision

ROD AND I took a big risk when we started our new venture. The great success that we now enjoy is due to our passionate belief and reliance on the fundamental principles of trusting our visions, and because we avoided listening to others. We also learned that partnerships in business can be very challenging; however, with both partners committed to the common goal and willing to appreciate what each brings to the table, partnerships can be an incredible avenue to success.

We need to ask ourselves who we want to be and what we want to contribute to the world. These fundamental questions set our sights on our vision for life. Your entrepreneurial life starts when you begin to practice the principles that underlie a simple but important truth: you create your success.

Education

IF YOU ARE young, a good way to approach your education is to enroll in a university that supports your vision and to approach each course as a lesson about self. Notice your resistance to certain courses and embrace the opportunity to grow and succeed in the face of your resistance. When you have a course you love, devote as much effort as you can to getting the most out of the content and context of the course. Look for the great "ah ha!" moments and always work on your personal growth, measuring your achievements in life against your vision, not your grades. In the end, what you believe about yourself is what you are going to create in the world. Your grades won't determine your level of financial success. If you graduate summa cum laude but you have an underlying belief that you don't deserve to make money or that highly successful people are fundamentally bad people, this belief will limit your success. In fact, even if you do have financial success, you will not feel the personal sense of fulfillment that you deserve. This is fundamental information, but most people never talk about it. Use these years to discover what lies within you and make the necessary changes in your belief systems to align them with your life's vision.

Don't Listen to Anybody Else

DON'T LISTEN TO others when it comes to your dreams and vision. The only person who can truly appreciate and understand your vision is you. It is your creation. In addition to not listening to others, you must block out your own internal negative thoughts.

You have what it takes to be successful, so just convince yourself of that fact and go from there. Spend quiet time with yourself and keep a journal about your thoughts, purpose, and vision. This will help you define how you really want your life to look, both personally and professionally. Keep writing and envisioning yourself, especially when you know that you are in a moment that expresses who you truly want to be.

Whatever path you choose, know that you will be growing personally and that you will be contributing to others as you grow your business. What is it that you bring to this world? Even if you don't consciously know the answer, a motivating force within you allows you to trust yourself and empower others. We are all unique, and so are our visions. My greatest quality, I believe, is my authenticity. My thoughts and actions are based on the fundamental principles that I share and teach. These principles are grounded in the truth that our thoughts create our experience and that I am the co-creator of my life. I love working with people and challenging them to discover their life's purpose and vision.

I've devoted much of my life to philanthropic endeavors, particularly in the area of animal protection. I've also found time to pursue my own personal dream to become an accomplished equestrian, winning numerous championship awards in the San Diego County show jumping circuit.

In these challenging economic times, it is essential that we get creative and find what we can bring to the table. In my case, I've used my real estate brokerage knowledge to launch a new business with my husband and my youngest son, Wes. The company is called Walz Equity Solutions, LLC, and it helps owners of seller-financed notes convert their note assets to needed cash.

Throughout the years, many books have inspired me, including Hope for the Flowers, Illusions: The Adventures of a Reluctant Messia), Friendship with God, and Power VS Force. These books explained so much to me that I decided to inspire others with my own book, Where's the Love? & Who's Got My Money? This book will guide you through your personal barriers so that you can find the romantic love you desire, whether you are seeking a new relationship or redefining the one you are in, and it will show you how to burst through your money barriers and create financial success in your life.

Focus and Metaphysics

WE CONSTANTLY SEE people who excel in almost everything they undertake. This may make you wonder, "Why them and not me?" However, chance has nothing to do with it. The reason these people are so successful is that they are highly focused. I attribute much of my success to my continued study of metaphysics. Metaphysical teachings state that by intensely focusing your expectation on a desired result, you realign the signal that you send out into the energy field that permeates everything within the universe. This signal then attracts energy that matches your projection of thought, resulting in the manifestation of the conditions you imagine. Scientific evidence has proven that expectancy and assumptions change our biochemistry.

Study

FOR THE PAST forty years, I have studied, applied, and taught the fundamental principle that you are already perfect, whole, and complete. Everything you need to create the life you desire and deserve is already within you, not without--your thoughts and beliefs combine to create the results in your life. More importantly, you can create whatever you desire into your life right now. My most prized protégé is my husband, Rod. Although he is gifted in many areas, his level money consciousness was very limited when we first met. His limiting beliefs had been poured into him by early childhood experiences and exposure, and I successfully coached him through them, resulting in an explosion of drive and creativity that led to enormous financial success. Numerous others have experienced breakthroughs and transformations in their personal and professional lives because of this coaching, which focuses on understanding, experiencing, and executing the fundamental success principles. The approach is specifically designed to burst through your inherited limiting beliefs so that you can create a life that actually puts you in control of your happiness, growth, and success.

Early Beliefs

IT IS CRITICAL to understand the relationship between your upbringing and your current level of success. Like my husband, many of you were exposed to parents, siblings, friends, and teachers early on who had limited and judgmental views of the world and financial success. Your underlying and inherited beliefs direct your focus and attention, so you need great concentration to overcome these limiting factors. Too often, people read an inspiring book and get motivated, but soon find themselves back to their past ways of limited thinking, believing their lack of success was due to external circumstances. Even our religions demand that we simply believe the principles we are taught, and discourage us from questioning these beliefs. Our internal belief system also operates in line with past thoughts. To paraphrase Einstein, you can't solve a problem with the same thinking that got you into it. It is no different with vision.

If you refuse to consider that your current set of beliefs may inhibit your vision, it's impossible for you to expand it. I cannot emphasize this enough. How many times have you heard about a lottery winner who blew through all their money and was left with nothing? These people have a fundamental belief that they are not worthy of the money or that people with money are different and they don't want to be like those people. Many people I encounter exhibit this limited thinking, but continue to complain that they are not successful and wonder what's standing in their way. A big key to success is becoming aware of these inherited limiting beliefs. I strongly recommend the PSI Seminars (www.psiseminars.com), an experiential weekend course that allows you to discover and confront your inherited beliefs.

Who we are and what we become is a direct reflection of our deeply embedded beliefs, and the longer you've held your limiting beliefs, the more committed you are to them. To replace negative, self-limiting thought patterns, you must focus on what it is you truly want to create in your life. Be gentle and patient with yourself, as this process may take time. Success comes naturally when you challenge your old thought patterns and focus on your vision.

You Are a Perfect
Expression of God

WITH A WELL-defined vision and purpose, you can set a plan in motion that prioritizes your focus, putting the most important things first. It is very easy to get caught up in activities that aren't moving you toward your vision, so refresh your vision and purpose periodically, reset your plan accordingly, and stay focused. Once I learned and practiced the principle that we are all perfect expressions of the One Infinite Power, the rest was easy. Get clear about what you want and truly believe that you deserve that life. You must be grateful every day for the knowledge that you are capable of achieving your dreams and you must give of yourself to others, from your heart, every day. Discover your true value and passion, get going, and never stop.

I love that I have been a part of something good and that I was able to contribute to the lives of my staff and to those of our clients as well. I am grateful that I have the opportunity to help people who are still struggling with the self-discovery process, and who haven't yet realized how great they are. I see people as they are in their truth, not how they show up. If they want to grow and are open to me, assisting them with their personal discovery is the most rewarding experience of my life.

We all have our own visions of how the perfect life would look. We each deserve to be fit and healthy, financially secure, living in the style we choose, and happy in a great relationship. The only thing that blocks us from reaching that realm is the belief that we don't deserve it. Changing your belief does require a new way of thinking about yourself. Master this, and you tap into the wonders of God and the blessings that follow. I know who you are in your truth; you are a perfect expression of God. When you acknowledge that truth, nothing will stop you.

Jeri Walz
Babe in Tweed

About Jeri Walz

JERI WALZ IS a successful businessperson, speaker and author who has inspired countless men and women to take charge of their lives and create results far beyond their expectations. Initially in the Real Estate Brokerage business, Jeri and her husband, Rod co-founded Walz Group which was recently named #45 in the Inc. 500 fastest growing companies and #4 of the top 100 service companies. Continuing to use her Real Estate Brokerage knowledge, Jeri, Rod, and their youngest son, Wes, launched Walz Equity Solutions, LLC. Because of her passion to support others creating success in their lives, Jeri is working on her first book, Where is the Love? & Who's Got My Money as well as starting Walz Success Seminars, designed to move people into a life of love, joy, health and financial prosperity.

COMPANY NAME: Walz Success Seminars

WEBSITE: www.walzsuccessseminars.com

EMAIL: jeri@walzgroup.com

BONUS GIFT:
I will send you a thought evoking questionnaire and include a 30 minute follow-up session to assist you moving forward in your life.

Babe in Tweed

Babe in Ivory

CHAPTER 5

Di Worrall:
Babe in Ivory

"Success is the progressive realization
of a worthy ideal."
—Earl Nightingale

I have been an out-of-the-box creative thinker from an early age. My creative and innovative spirit was fueled by a fierce need for independence, a powerful combination for entrepreneurial pursuits. The entrepreneur in me had to wait, however. The most influential years of my early life were spent entirely immersed in the conformist paradigm—my family, my education, and my first working experiences in the public sector all reinforced this frame of reference.

Over the course of twenty years, I advanced to various senior executive positions within large public and private sector organizations. From the beginning of my career, I was conscious of a whisper in the back of my mind calling me to embrace my entrepreneurial spirit. During this twenty-year period, the whisper steadily grew to eventually become a shout, which I could no longer ignore. The shout turned out to be a strong paradigm shift. Today,

I am driven by my progress toward achieving my highest goals, not by expending a specific amount of time on certain activities in the traditional sense of work. I may not be there yet, but my ultimate goal is to become Chief Entrepreneurial Officer (CEO), where my desire to work outweighs any specific need to work, and I am free to focus on my greatest strengths and delegate the work that is outside my preferences.

Shortly after my decision to become an entrepreneur, I took the position that to be successful, a business had to uncover a unique competitive advantage. I looked carefully for ways to distinguish myself, and I discovered the following attributes:

- My Message: I am driven to open the door to everything that's possible in our lives, our communities, and our businesses. I help people answer the question: How can we open the door to a climate for change?

- My Experience: By working with me or studying my materials, you'll hear stories of my real experiences, which include the glories of success and the war stories of failure. I have experienced, managed, studied, and advised on change as an entrepreneur, author, social commentator, corporate leader, and employee.

- My Perspective: Though some might consider a highly paid successful senior executive to be the pinnacle of success, I chose to give up that identity and security. Based on the strength of a vision, I started again from scratch as an entrepreneur. Audiences won't get a college lecture; they'll get the reality show.

THE MAIN DIFFERENCE between my life as an entrepreneur and my life in the corporate world is best described by the Pareto Principle, or 80/20 rule. As an executive, I spent 80 percent of my time on activities that the organization required, and only the remaining 20 percent on activities that energized and revitalized me. I valued the psychic space that non-work time afforded to recover, regroup, and re-energize for the next workday. A driving force behind my decision to transition from corporate life to the entrepreneurial experience was to do more of what I loved. Now,

I am close to spending 80 percent of my time doing what I love and 20 percent on what needs to be done to run the business. This transition was possible because of a crystal clear focus, and the willingness to embrace a virtual workforce through outsourcing where it made sense.

As an entrepreneur, it can be challenging to differentiate work from many non-work activities. My last executive role required 80 work hours a week, with a large volume of "have to" or "should do" activities. This pattern extended over many years and took its toll on my personal, social, and family life, as well as my professional networking opportunities. With the wisdom of hindsight, I was living a paradox. While I experienced the power, influence, and trappings of executive life, I was also experiencing the disempowerment of subsuming my personal goals to those of the business.

Having experienced the paradigm that the structure and culture of corporate life is the "right" way to do things, I initially assumed this work pattern when I opened my own business. My mentors soon challenged this model, but it was a while before I could move past my learned feelings of guilt. I eventually came to terms with the knowledge that my natural rhythms are not suited to a 9 to 5 framework, and that work doesn't have to occur within any predetermined daily block of time to be effective. Once I embraced this new paradigm, I felt a renewed sense of focus, energy, and enjoyment, which blurred the line between work and non-work activities. Since my experience of work is determined and purposeful, I don't need nearly as much psychic recovery time to prepare for my next challenge. I engage in far fewer activities in the "have to" category, so work doesn't feel like work and has nowhere near the same drain on my energy or the same impact on my friends and family. Another benefit of being an entrepreneur is that I'm free to network professionally. The guilt of "having" to be somewhere is gone, so I'm able to attend events and functions that I wish to attend with more frequency and vitality.

I start every day with intention, reminding myself of my highest goals and priorities. I find this simple habit absolutely vital because if I'm not focused, my time can be hijacked by the priorities of other people. For this same reason, it is essential to properly manage e-mail. In the morning, I resist the urge to open my inbox right away because I know there are several e-mails from people wanting something from me. Instead, the first thing I do is reinforce my two or three top priorities for that day.

On days I travel out of the office, I listen to CDs or read educational or inspirational material, such as interviews of fascinating people or seminars and presentations. I used to just listen to radio news and music, but I stopped doing this some time ago and have never looked back. Stop for a moment and think about all the time we waste on unimportant activities during our commute to and from work. This is time we can never get back. What would happen if we repurposed this time with the aim of bettering ourselves and opening doors to new opportunities? Timothy Ferriss, author of The 4-Hour Workweek, is spot-on when he challenges readers to develop the skill of being selectively ignorant. "The first step is to develop and maintain a low information diet…Most information is time-consuming, negative, irrelevant to your goals, and outside of your influence."

Spending two hours a day listening to empowering, energizing, and uplifting messages that are in sync with your goals and objectives amounts to at least ten weeks of full-time study, customized to your personal needs, over the course of a year! In the words of Eric Hoffer, "In times of change, learners inherit the earth, while the learned find themselves beautifully equipped for a world that no longer exists."

When I'm not meeting with clients, business partners, the media or conducting seminars, I use the morning to take care of practical, pragmatic activities. In the middle of the day, I'll break and socialize, network, or read. The afternoons and evening are reserved for more creative pursuits; for example, I find that I write best in the late afternoons, then again from later in the evening and occasionally into the early hours of the morning. This pattern best suits my personal style. Other colleagues reverse this pattern, and attend to their creative tasks in the morning and their more practical or administrative tasks later in the day. I always end the evening with personal reflections on the day, a reminder of what

I plan for the following day, and a deliberate effort to be grateful for every experience of the day. I'm not trying to describe an unattainably perfect day in a fantasy life; I still get distracted, I focus on what went wrong, I obsess over my inadequacies, and I stray off my purpose, but it's okay. As long as I keep an optimistic attitude, everything will soon fall back into place.

While I did get a buzz out of the corporate experience, I functioned as though I had no choice but to focus all of my energy on protecting my career while advancing someone else's business goals, and my personal relationships took second billing. The beauty of the entrepreneurial experience is that I can now choose to spend as much or as little time as I want with friends and family. While spending time with family and friends is important, it's not always my highest priority. I deeply appreciate the advice of my friends and family and realize it comes from the best of intentions, but I have realized that the only person who knows what is best for me is me. I always consider the views of my loved ones, but I balance them against the advice of mentors and supporters and, most importantly, my own intuition.

The beautiful truth is that the challenges and advice offered by our loved ones are a blessing in disguise. My goals don't always fall inside the parameters of their comfort zones, and therein lies a challenge. One of the reasons I decided to leave corporate life and go into my own business was because of the advice of my friends and family, but my closest advocates morphed into the expression of my gravest personal doubts, outlining everything that could go wrong. This served to allow me to confront my fears rather than hide behind them. While it's true that things don't always go according to plan in a new venture, I now take the position that my highest goals are the ultimate expression of my path and are true for me.

While I am flexible about shifting the path I choose to achieve a particular objective, the end goal is unmoving. A select few of my highest professional goals carry a personal resolve that never wavers. This comes from a certainty that exceeds anyone else's doubt. For example, I decided to write a book titled *A Climate for Change*. My closest family and friends thought it was an interesting and exciting project, yet couldn't help but share their opinion that the book might not be good enough to publish. Their response stemmed from fear for me, specifically out of love and concern that exposure to public scrutiny could hurt or embarrass me.

Nevertheless, my goal to write this book was so strong that I held tight to my vision. While many of our fears are of an imaginary future, some of them may in fact come to pass. Indeed, this has been my experience throughout the writing and publishing process. I've felt the unsettling sting of criticism from strangers who have challenged my views, but I have also moved past this to discover the silver lining. These challenges taught me that by moving forward, I become more resilient, and this has opened the door to new marketing, PR, and joint venture opportunities that I hadn't seen before. On the flip side, I've relished the positive and enthusiastic feedback from people whose lives and careers have been taken to a new level because of my material and coaching.

If We Don't Change the Way We Think, How Can We Expect Different Results?

MY MOST CRUCIAL entrepreneurial experience was finding the courage to confront and challenge the attitudes that were limiting the expression of my highest personal and professional goals. My earlier example of lottery winners shows just how much attitude and self-image design the outcome of our lives. Research has indicated that only a small minority of lottery winners maintained their winnings—the vast majority ended up worse off than before. Without challenging the part of their self-image that determined their self-worth, their unconscious patterns of behavior went into overdrive to return them to the financial position that was consistent with their self-image.

The lottery analysis is not just a statistic for me. About fifteen years ago, my ex-husband and I won first prize in an Australian lottery. At that time, our mindset focused on consumption rather than investment. In a short period of time our winnings were consumed by what we thought was a sensible strategy—pay off debt, buy some little luxuries, and have a holiday. Even the simplest strategy of investing ten percent and reinvesting the interest would have produced a respectable yield a little more than a decade later.

Years later, when I began my entrepreneurial journey, my initial goals were to work less, to do more of what I really enjoyed doing (creating, coaching, and change consulting), and to earn the same income as when I was a senior executive. Compared to the experience of many other first-time entrepreneurs, my scorecard is good. I achieved all three goals in varying degrees: I spend at least 40 percent less time working, I am much more time engaged in what I really enjoy doing, and I earn as much as I did in corporate life.

Outwardly, I was pleased with this result, but inwardly, I felt that such an enormous change in my business and lifestyle should be offering something more. Around that time, I attended a conference where Bob Proctor was the featured presenter. Over dinner, Bob, a wealthy entrepreneur and master coach, asked me, "What do you do and how much did you earn last year?" I proudly announced that in the first year of business in my own change management consultancy, I earned exactly the same amount as I did as a senior executive at a large corporation.

"Well, that's rubbish," he replied. His response was startling. He then said, "From this instant, stop trading your time for money, or else go back to corporate life." Although I can't say I expected this response, his words resonated with that underlying feeling that there must be something more to all this. In that instant, I knew he was absolutely right.

Bob's advice changed the course of my life from that point forward. I soon became aware that by earning the same annual income in my first foray into entrepreneurial life as I had in corporate life, I was acting out a habitual pattern based on my deepest values and beliefs about my self-image. My self-image had defined what I was worth and the lifestyle that goes with that value. It led me to the opportunities that produced my entrepreneurial income and the associated lifestyle, habits, and networks that were consistent with the self-image I'd carefully cultivated over decades in the corporate world. While achieving some success as an entrepreneur, this self-image also set out the limiting beliefs that caused me to unconsciously sabotage any opportunity that would cause my business to grow beyond this self-imposed ceiling. I was acting out my unconscious habit patterns.

I made the decision to challenge my thoughts, and lift the ceiling of my limiting beliefs about who I am, what I do, and how much I earn. With continuous work reinforced by deliberate visualization, affirmations, weekly goal setting, and a good coach, I've made significant breakthroughs in how I value myself and my business. One of the thoughts I challenged was my ability to write a book. I procrastinated over this fantasy for over twenty years, but a chance meeting with a publisher changed all that. With a renewed commitment to lifting the lid off the possibilities of my business, I was asked a simple question about writing my book: "Would now be a good time?" This was another of those defining moments that obliterated any and all excuses I harbored. It was a call to action and without hesitation, I was ready to answer the call. That one decision opened doors for me that I didn't even know existed. *A Climate for Change: How to Ride the Wave of Change into the 21st Century* spawned new business opportunities, joint ventures, new networks, media opportunities, and even spurred a new line of business based on the book.

A Climate for Change and other books in the Creating a Climate for Change series now in the pipeline are a 21st century expression of my business of advice and support. It represents an evolution in the way my business and I can be of service using a fast and efficient way to touch the lives of as many people as possible. I hope it will leave a legacy that many people will find of value in years to come.

My self-image is rarely haunted by the spectra of senior executive life anymore. My business has become less about conforming to a particular image and more about ways I can serve my customers. I've enjoyed redesigning my business to match market needs with my strengths. I've done this by creating a unique range of services and products, a strategy that goes a long way toward eliminating competition. While I have far-reaching financial and business goals, it's the smaller goals that keep me motivated to keep going.

THE QUOTE AT the beginning of this chapter is one of my favorites. Success is not the destination, goal, or end state. Rather, it is the journey and sense of purpose that causes us to take one step after the other. This is the heart of the definition. Success isn't the same for everyone, and the hopes and goals that inspire our priorities change over the course of our lives and some may be more important than others, depending on the stage we're at. I find that the first step in creating your model of success is to examine all the different aspects of your life, beyond just work and family, and decide which are the most important to you now and in your immediate future. Create a short list. Next, decide on the goals you want to achieve based on the items in that shortlist. Here is a model of how you might categorize the diversity of your life. Of course, you can create this model any way that makes sense to you.

I've listed some of the most important lessons I learned about achieving my goals as an entrepreneur below:

- Progress toward goals is counted in each little step I take toward their completion.

- We can never know how long it will take or the precise path to follow to achieve the full expression of our goal.

- Release the need to control, and work with the direction your path is taking you.

- When starting new projects, I need to be generous with my timelines and budget, cut through the non-essentials, and take time out to master new skills.

- If I find myself blaming other people or circumstances, or find myself experiencing the same setback time and time again, I am probably not handling that particular failure very well.

Some essential lessons I've learned on my journey are:

- Discover your strengths and weaknesses, and how they can catapult you forward or how they are holding you back.

- Identify your highest goals and priorities and review them regularly.

- Appoint business and life coaches/mentors.

- Learn the difference between a job and the process of creating wealth from the masters, and start applying these lessons today.

- Learn to accept that failure is not something to be avoided. Rather, failure is a form of feedback to be celebrated as a precious key that can teach you the next step toward fulfilling your goals.

VERY FEW PEOPLE have the skills to start something and the skills to finish it in equal measure. I find it important to recognize whether you are a natural starter or finisher and discipline yourself to achieve mastery in the other (or find someone who complements your skill set). Highly creative people often start projects with great energy and enthusiasm, but sabotage their success with their aversion to completion. Others might be reluctant to act on a new opportunity, but be very adept at driving a project to its conclusion.

The capacity to recognize and take action on opportunity is a key strategic advantage. Business success can often be attributed to being the first out of the starting gate, not necessarily the best. If you can't connect with the market however, it doesn't matter whether you're the first or last out of the gate. It is crucial to identify your market, empathize with them, give them what they want, and keep them coming back for more.

Creativity is also essential for your path to success. For me, generating ideas is as natural as breathing. My thinking style works best in the creative and innovative mindset. I have been known to write creatively for up to five or six hours without a break. Clearly, generating new ideas is not an issue for me. My challenge is the discipline of capturing those ideas and prioritizing them. I'm okay with this. Many entrepreneurs, including Bill Gates, have similar thinking and working styles. I've listed the methods I use to ensure I move my ideas into purposeful action below:

- Remind myself of my highest goals and my short-term plans to reach them.

- Use beautiful notebooks to capture and record ideas for my businesses and for my books. (This gives the ideas the precious status they deserve).

- Read books, listen to audio, and watch visual media on subjects related to my goals, and read and write notes in cafes and restaurants where I can concentrate well.

- Quiet my mind and meditate before sitting down to an intense session of book or article writing.

- Attend seminars and networking events regularly.

- Budget for and spend money on personal development.

- Set artificial parameters like deadlines and financial milestones.

- Get a goal coach to contain my idea generation, address procrastination, and cause me to take action.

- Outsource the tasks that are necessary to move forward, but that I don't need to personally master.

IF WE ARE more oriented toward either the creative or the pragmatic way of approaching work, how do we offset the potential blind spots this may cause in our business? If we choose not to outsource immediately, there is a way of stimulating the parts of our brain that we don't use as frequently. The right side of our brain is where we uncover unusual and creative solutions to problems. The use of a mind map can stimulate our creative thoughts. It works by identifying a goal and then describing all the different pathways to achieve that goal. We use the left side of our brain for logical and analytical thinking. We can stimulate our brain to operate this way by assessing the value or merits of a proposal.

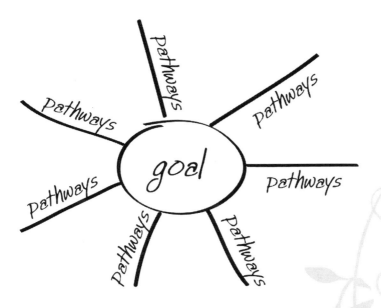

TEAMS CAN ALSO be plagued by these blind spots. If you are a no-nonsense, practical, and pragmatic person, you are likely to be drawn to people who are also pragmatic. If you're an entrepreneur or a corporate manager who hires staff, your comfort level around people with this way of thinking might cause you to hire pragmatic people over others who have a more annoying, creative bent. Therefore, when it comes to business decisions, you and your team might see things in a similar way and make the same good judgments, but also make the same mistakes and miss the same opportunities to innovate.

Right - and left - brain thinking techniques can also be applied in groups of people. A popular technique to encourage a group to activate the creative right side of its thinking is the brainstorming technique. Using this technique, each member of the group is asked to offer a solution to a problem or pathway to a goal. The rule is that every suggestion is encouraged and accepted without question.

Analyzing those suggestions then needs the support of left-brain activity. A left-brain analysis might narrow the suggestions down into a priority list from one through three, where one is the highest priority idea and three is the lowest. Focusing on the high priorities, the analysis could be further refined by applying several more levels of assessment criteria, for example, cost/benefit analysis. I use these techniques often, and they successfully achieve better solutions to business goals.

Life as an entrepreneur can be full of setbacks, especially for someone like me, who had little entrepreneurial experience before opening for business. My previous experience in project management was on a large scale with the support of a corporate budget, infrastructure, and battery of expert resources. This doesn't exactly translate easily into entrepreneurial life, where I often underestimated how much time and money it took to complete an unfamiliar project. An important aspect of dealing with these experiences was my willingness to take responsibility, accept them as a normal and natural part of the learning process, and give myself permission to change whatever wasn't working. These experiences gave me a new opportunity to handle failure and have some fun with it.

It has been a steep learning curve both personally and professionally, but it's definitely been worthwhile, as it gave me a new foundation from which to move forward. Everything I have experienced has come into my life for a reason, both good and bad. I wouldn't have the business, leadership, and change management credibility. I currently enjoy, if I hadn't worked in the corporate world, enjoyed some major success, and made some spectacular mistakes along the way.

Di Worrall
Babe in Ivory

About Di Worrall

DI WORRALL, the Principal of Worrall & Associates: Strategic HR and Change Consulting, has over twenty years of experience leading strategic change. With postgraduate qualifications in change from the Australian Graduate School of Management (AGSM), her change initiatives have touched the lives of over twenty-five thousand people and helped organizations unravel the fundamental drivers of lasting change. In her book, *A Climate for Change,* along with her signature seminars and keynotes offer her insights into the secrets of successfully riding the wave of change into the twenty-first century. With her vast experience as a consultant, coach, author, presenter, and social commentator, she is a champion of creating opportunities for high performance. Di's expertise will help you discover what works, what doesn't, and how to make the necessary changes to correct the situation.

COMPANY NAME: Worrall & Associates

WEBSITE: www.humanresourceschange.com.au

EMAIL: di@humanresourceschange.com.au

BONUS GIFT:
FREE audio download - *"How to turn obstacles into opportunities"*
at www.humanresourceschange.com.au/book

Babe in Black

CHAPTER 6

Marianne Ford: Babe in Black

"It's not how much you know, but how much you can inspire others to learn what you know."

— Marianne Ford

Years ago when I was teaching, I was invited to a Mary Kay Cosmetics party. I think I was just curious and I went because the consultant was an old friend of the family. I didn't use skin care products or make-up, and I definitely didn't do the "party thing." Nevertheless, my impressions of these Mary Kay women suggested that they were very confident and well put together, so why not me? Unfortunately, I kept my confidence well hidden at the party, and no one came up to me and said, "You know, Marianne, you'd be great at this!" In fact, the consultant, sensing my lack of confidence, leaned over and whispered, "I think you need this, dear!" "It would be good for you!" Even so, several years passed before I seriously thought about going into business for myself. I didn't love what I was doing, and my paycheck was definitely not enough.

The truth is, I kind of liked the look of the glamorous Mary Kay life. I eventually quit my teaching job, made a commitment to go to the top, and never looked back. From my very first day in business, my goal was to earn a pink Cadillac, and elevate myself to the highest position in the company. I was absolutely passionate about it. There was no question in my mind that I could do it, and I had a plan. I sought out the most successful women in the business—the ones who had what I wanted—and followed their instruction and mentoring, without question. I didn't need to reinvent the wheel, I just did the work! It never really crossed my mind that I was becoming an "entrepreneur," I just wanted to work my own hours and make money.

I was totally unaware of the concept of personal growth, because it wasn't commonly spoken about back then, and if you referred to the Laws of Nature and Attraction or the universe, you were labeled New Age and not taken seriously. Actually, I had no idea that I had so much to learn! I just went to work with determination, persistence, and courage. That was over twenty-five years ago. Mary Kay laid the foundation, and helped me build the knowledge that I would later use to start my own speaking business when many of my contemporaries were thinking of retirement.

It's difficult for me to name one skill that is necessary for achieving success. There are so many skills to be learned along the way, such as strong presentation skills, marketing, negotiating, handling objections, technology, networking, leadership, and priority management. I believe that I can narrow it down, however, to three major components: commitment, conscious choice, and communication.

Commitment

THE FIRST COMPONENT of commitment is knowing exactly what you want, and being passionately committed to that crystal clear goal. This single most important attribute will make up for deficiencies in all the other areas. It will allow you to win in life no matter what obstacles you encounter. Commitment gives you the power and focus to overcome every challenge and setback you will face along your path to achieving your goals, in every area of your life.

When committed, your focus automatically prioritizes the most important activities for each day. These activities will make a difference in whether or not your goals will be reached, and believe me, it's not about having a clean desk! The priority in this industry is always new business. Who do you have to call, write, or introduce yourself to? The underlying principle of this message is that if you are out of new contacts, you are out of business. Commitment keeps you on track, regardless of what is happening around you. Commitment also propels you forward to success and achievement and drives you to action in every area. The lack or presence of commitment in your life determines whether you will be a failure or a success. Each one of us has the ability to commit to a goal, a project, or a relationship—it's a choice we make.

To be able to move forward even when everything around you is collapsing, and meeting challenges face on, takes real courage. My definition of someone with personal leadership and professionalism is someone who keeps going no matter what, even when it's really tough, or when circumstances bring us to our knees. Many of us know what we need to do, yet we don't take action. We succumb to our emotions, or we spend our time looking for the quick fix that will change our lives, rather than using commitment and courage to move forward, step by step, toward the finish line. Before you can commit, however, you need to identify what it is you want. This takes some introspection and journaling. Not only do you have to visualize your success picture, but you also have to experience the feeling associated with the achievement. What will it feel like to have financial freedom, your dream home, the best of health, the perfect relationship, or peace of mind? Draw a picture; make a list. Be as specific as possible when creating your vision, and affirm yourself several times a day.

That means picking two or three of your best qualities, or two or three qualities you want to possess, and saying them passionately, aloud. For example, "I speak with confidence in every situation," or, "I attract incredibly positive people and situations every day." Act as if you are the person you want to be, and you are living the life you really want. At this point, it just takes discipline to focus on the required actions necessary to make your dream come true. Remember, the dream is the big picture and the action is the step-by-step completion of daily goals. Set your goals for the next day before you go to bed, and check them off as you complete them throughout the day. It takes discipline, focus, and consistent work to achieve anything worthwhile.

Successful people don't have the word failure in their dictionary. They turn every situation into a learning experience. Remove the word failure from your vocabulary, and replace it with the word lesson. As your commitment increases, you will become unstoppable. You will love what you do, who you are, and who you are becoming. It won't feel like work. Your positive energy will attract the people and things you have visualized and asked for. You will sense your value to the universe increase and feel it make a difference to everyone around you. Your purpose and commitment will fuel your motivation, no matter how long the journey is, or how many times you may have to adjust the date of your goals.

Conscious Choices

WE MAY SOMETIMES think we have no choices, but the reality is that we always do. To recognize those choices and to respond positively, it is necessary to become aware of negative patterns of behavior and break the cycle. We must learn to identify when we are self-sabotaging or creating negative self-talk, both of which are hugely detrimental to achieving success. Feelings of anger, judgment, guilt, and blame are disempowering, and lead to emotional distress. Your motivation vanishes and the quest for your dream is lost. Learn how to notice when you are going down the wrong road and learn to switch gears. It's a process. Once you've identified a behavior pattern you want to change, try to notice each time you start going down that old road and change your thoughts before they play out into the old behavior patterns. Soon the noticing will become a habit, and new positive behavior will take its place.

We have choices. We don't have to go through life letting people or situations control us, or we them. We all have infinite possibilities at our disposal. Your thoughts provide an image, and through conscious choice, thoughts, and intention, you grow it into reality. The choices we make determine the quality of our lives. Choose to view your struggles and frustrations as possibilities, not obstacles, and make sure you surround yourself with people who enhance your best qualities.

With any choice that you make, you may have to make adjustments to your course, but your focus needs to stay the same. Your choices build your character, unlock your imagination and creativity, and enable you to reap the benefits. The freedom that making conscious choices grants you will create a confidence that empowers you to move forward. Whether any given choice is right or wrong, it will be a definite learning experience, and our lives are built one experience at a time. Consciously choosing your actions allows you to take responsibility for their outcome. Things aren't just happening to you anymore—they're happening because of you. Your success depends upon choosing effectively.

Keep in mind that timing is everything. If something must be done today and you don't do it, you'll often get that nagging feeling of "I should have," or that you have failed in some way. On one hand, you are always given more chances; however, you'll never know what might have resulted from taking action now. We'll never understand the intricate workings of all the forces in the universe that move on our behalf. Much may be depending on completing each task and achieving each goal today, and just one action may be the very one that opens the door of opportunity. If you neglect to move quickly, it may be a while before you get what you want.

You can make every action strong and effective by holding a vision of it while you are performing it, and focusing on that vision. Seize and enjoy your moments! With practice, you will be able to separate mental power from personal action. If all of your mental power goes into every action, no matter how commonplace, every action will be a success in itself. It's about being present, or being consciously in the moment. In accordance with the Laws of Attraction, every success opens the way to other successes, and your progress toward what you want, as well as what you want to attract, will become increasingly rapid. Each day is filled with challenges, and your response to those challenges determines how successful you will be that particular day.

Communication

THE THIRD CRUCIAL element to success is developing great communication skills. The most important person you need to talk to, hear, and understand is yourself. The more at home you are with that person, the easier it will be to communicate with everyone else. What do you like? What don't you like? What are your triggers? What makes you happy, sad, excited, or angry? Get honest with yourself. Peel back the layers, especially when negative emotions are involved, and find out where they came from. Negative behavior patterns continually create fear-based reactions, which may have absolutely nothing to do with the situation or person in front of you today. Unfortunately, those actions can change the course of your life forever.

We all have response–ability. We also react, over and over again, which prevents us from learning new lessons. Reaction has no thought to it—it's instantaneous. If it's explosive, it's called a trigger. Triggers set off or initiate exaggerated emotional behavior and reactions. The feelings caused by triggers feel ugly. They cause withdrawal, lashing out, total unrest in the body, and the waste of precious quality time, not to mention the diseases caused by anxiety. There can be no positive outcome to a conversation when a person is in a "triggered state." Take a break and wait for the feeling to pass, whether you or someone else is having the reaction.

This is your "stuff," and it takes a lot of awareness and work to get through and into a new place of understanding. Welcome the people in your life who push your buttons, because they are crucial in promoting your personal growth. You probably never thought of it that way before, but it's true! It's your choice to learn to deal with their presence. Just keep chanting to yourself that your "stuff" and your reactions are all about you not about them. They have their own "stuff," which they may or may not be aware of. Blame on either side is unacceptable.

Responding, in contrast to reacting, is grounded, accepting, and non-judgmental. Communicating with others involves hearing and understanding, not working on your righteous rebuttal. Good communication is based on listening so that you can understand the other person's view. It's not about being right or having the last word. It's about accepting that someone else may have an opinion that differs from yours and understanding that it doesn't mean it's wrong. Remember that controlling your reactions is a skill that would probably bring world peace if everyone could do it!

A lack of basic communication skills severely impedes your success in all aspects of your life. By basics, I mean not interrupting, but truly focusing on what the other person is saying, and asking for clarification before you respond. Negative emotion needs to be held in check, and you need to go to a neutral state if you're trying to gather information. Silence can be very golden! That's not to say that you can't scream and shout and beat pillows when you are alone. That in itself is very therapeutic, and promotes healing and growth.

Sometimes, we don't want a solution. Sometimes, we just want to be heard, but so does everyone else—it's a basic human need. Unfortunately, everyone has an opinion that they want to share. Take the high road and be the person who doesn't always have to give it!

We all have to learn our own lessons. Instead of always trying to fix situations or offer opinions, we need to allow ourselves to come to our own conclusions, decisions, and choices with no judgment, and enable others to do the same. It's a difficult lesson and it takes a great deal of emotional maturity to learn it. Realize that this is a journey, and that changing and sustaining new thought patterns and beliefs is not an overnight process.

You will always be in contact with people going through their own processes, whether consciously or unconsciously, and you will learn from your interactions with them, as will they. This journey is about becoming present, clear, and non-defensive. Clear communication takes the guesswork out of relationships, clarifies misunderstandings, diminishes resentment and frustration, and promotes balance.

To effectively communicate, it is vital that you know, explore, and understand your needs and desires first. Engaging in self-reflection will clarify your needs and desires, and ultimately ease communication and reduce misinterpretation. You'll be more comfortable, direct, and authentic when you know what you want and how you want to say it. Lack of clarity often leads to a breakdown in communication and understanding, which will have a negative impact on any interaction.

Another reason communication can sometimes feel awkward is that you are opening yourself up to the truth and displaying how you really feel. There is always a risk of being judged or criticized, but confrontation is never necessary. Replace confrontation with discussion, which allows you to deal with the issue and move forward.

Step out of your comfort zone and ask for what you want, no matter what it is. If you don't, years from now, you'll regret not speaking up. Great communication puffs people up and makes them feel that something wonderful has just happened. By understanding your own issues first, you can avoid feeling resentful and hurt. Bear in mind that you have to be patient—not everyone is consciously aware of their contribution to a situation, or of their responsibility in arriving at a resolution. While your communication skills develop, they still may be in "blame" mode. Persevere by continually working on yourself.

In most cases, your energy will be contagious, but there will always be people who refuse to acknowledge and change their bad habits. In these cases, know that you can't change another person. Let it go! Use open-ended questions to retrieve more information. Use "I" statements that help you take ownership of how you feel, and allow you to be clear about what you need, without using language that is accusatory or blaming. Your focus should always be on the solution.

Respecting a relationship means that you can listen to the other person's thoughts and feelings and demonstrate that you value the relationship, even when you disagree with them. Listening shows that you genuinely care. When you disagree, maintain open channels of communication by saying, "I really appreciate you taking the time to work this out with me," or by reiterating what they've said to ensure that you've received the message correctly. It always amazes me how one story can have so many different interpretations.

Keep in mind that we approach communication from a place of either love or fear. Fear is always negatively based. Emotional responses such as control, anger, depression, regret, loneliness, worry, and judgment all come from fear. They all "talk" too much and take up too much space. Train yourself to come from a place of love, which is joy, happiness, acceptance, and peace. Never presume that you know what others are thinking, as the stories we create in our minds are far more destructive than reality. Even in business, many people over-talk the sale, and usually lose it as a result. Talking too much clouds your presence and makes you look needy. Ask questions, and really listen to the responses. People want to do business with confident, enthusiastic, joyful, and authentic people. Be one.

The more unconscious baggage you let go of, the more authentic you become. It almost feels as though you're melting into yourself. As you learn to communicate effectively, your fears begin to fall away and your emotional self starts to grow up, and catching up with the rest of you! A new confidence and contentment will take over as you discover that there is rarely a need to react, when responding is so much more effective. What a great level of awareness to strive for!

At my seminars, when I ask people what their biggest obstacle is, the response is overwhelmingly the same thing: MYSELF! Well, now you know how to get over yourself, and focus on what's really important: what you want, where you are going, and who you're going to take with you.

My life and career experiences have taken me on an incredible personal journey, and I hope the wisdom I've gained inspires you to follow your dreams. I've inspired myself from within over and over again, not because I have a large ego, but because I've had to. I learned long ago that no one else is coming to my rescue! I'm astounded at my resilience and my inner strength, which continues to be tested. I've had to endure and overcome the misconceptions that I wasn't working a "real" job, and today, direct sales and multi-level marketing have grown to monumental proportions, supporting and employing millions of people all over the world, and positively changing countless lives!

I am one of those lives, and this journey has provided me with wisdom, extraordinary experiences, and unprecedented personal growth. Our lives are ongoing journeys and they are full of unpredictable chapters. Decide what you want, commit to it, and welcome the learning that comes from the challenging lessons you'll encounter on your way.

Marianne Ford
Babe in Black

About Marianne Ford:

MARIANNE has been a highly successful speaker and facilitator in the Direct Sales Industry for the last 25 years. She left her teaching career to earn 4 Pink Cadillac's with Mary Kay Cosmetics. She went on to be the Corporate Director of Sales for two multi-million dollar Direct Sales Companies, plus has become a very popular and highly successful corporate "change" advisor and speaker. She has recorded the "Magic Business", and "Change Your Thinking, Change Your Life CD". Her expertise includes being a Licensed facilitator of Stephen Covey's, "The 7 Habits of Highly Effective People" She also and is the founder of MUMS – Mothers Unite against MS.

FULL NAME: Marianne Ford

COMPANY NAME: Marianne Ford Seminars

WEBSITE:www.marianneford.com

EMAIL: marianne@marianneford.com

BONUS GIFT
$100 off your first coaching session.

Babe in Black

Babe in Pink

CHAPTER 7

Sherry Wilsher: Babe in Pink

"First comes thought; then organization of that thought into ideas and plans; then transformation of those plans into reality. The beginning, as you will observe, is in your imagination."

— **Napoleon Hill**

My entire life is built on imagination. If you can master this skill, knowledge will be attracted to you. I spent years looking for that perfect job or position, but to no avail. Most of my career had been spent in the dental field, and although I enjoyed creating beautiful smiles on my imaging computer and helping create them in the operation room, I always felt like there was something more for me. Finally, after twelve years, I left and went into real estate.

My experiences in dentistry and real estate were major precursors to what I am building today. During my time in dentistry, I was always trying to invent something that would make me millions. I even thought of writing a book to share my computer imaging knowledge, but never moved forward with it. My real estate career immediately established a feeling of accomplishment, it provided a higher income level than I had achieved in dentistry, and it acted as another step up the ladder of my success.

Because I always wanted more, I studied many books including, *The Success Principles, Happy for No Reason, and Think and Grow Rich.* These books helped me find and fulfill my life's purpose, and I believe that anyone who wants to clarify their mission and purpose should read *The Success Principles,* particularly if they are interested in creating a successful business. Happy for No Reason taught me the importance of maintaining the happiness set-point, which is the level of happiness you need to sustain to receive life's true blessings. I strongly encourage you to study these books as I did.

My past reading and learning spawned more and more thoughts about achieving my own success, and gave me the ability to dream even bigger than ever, creating the life of abundance that I now enjoy, and that is available to all who seek it.

Focused Intention

IN 2001, I was living in a small home with very little space for all of my personal care items. I was always throwing things under the sink and placing miscellaneous items in makeshift bins. I was notorious for leaving my items at arm's length for convenience, but my neat freak side was always nudging me to tidy up. The result was that everything would end up in the cabinet under the bathroom sink, along with all the plumbing and other miscellaneous items. Another challenge I faced was when my husband would come into the bathroom during my morning routine to shower and steam up the whole room, ruining any chances of a good hair day.

I decided to make my life a little easier by purchasing a cart at a discount store and placing plastic bins in the wire racks to accommodate my "beauty stuff," which included all of my makeup, my hair dryer, curling irons, and styling products, among other things. I was so pleased with the set-up that I ended up using it for several years. One day I was dreaming aloud with my girlfriends and I told them about my idea, which now included several upgrades. They both said, "That's an awesome idea!"

I thought about it for a moment, but my lack of ambition and fear of the unknown caused me to let it go.

While reading the book, *Think and Grow Rich* by Napoleon Hill, the thought of my incredible makeup cart came back to me. With a fresh burst of inspiration, combined with what I learned from Napoleon Hill, I immediately recognized this huge opportunity and started searching for any other products that might already exist that were similar and found none. This was truly it – the idea that could launch my own success!

I am the creator of the Caddy by SleekaVi©, a vanity cart that held everything a person could want right at their fingertips. The cart is sleek in design and offers electrical outlets and holding devises for styling products. It offers drawers for an assortment of personal care products, and the top drawers are constructed with dividers to keep lipsticks, eye makeup, foundations, and more, in an organized space, while the remaining drawers are designed to store brushes, combs, styling products, and accessories.

Inspiration

EVERY ONCE IN a while, you meet someone who inspires you. They exude enthusiasm and genuinely care about what they are doing, the people with whom they work, and the people they serve. They express a joy that seems to come from deep within; it's not forced or superficial. You sense their genius and authenticity, and you don't believe they are playing a role.

I look around at all the greatness that surrounds me and I am inspired to keep moving forward every day. So often, we only hear about the success of people in the media, but I like to discover the story behind the great successes stories. I like to hear about the road they traveled in their path to riches. Rags-to-riches stories inspire me so much, and remind me that anyone can achieve greatness.

Fulfillment comes from the inside out, not the other way around. Finding the greatness within you is a spiritual quest that represents your ability to connect with something greater than yourself. Isn't that what we all want to do—make a difference in the lives of others and leave a legacy behind? None of us wants to think that we will live and die without leaving any meaningful trace of ourselves.

The word passion is often used to describe your purpose. Passion is about a feeling deep inside. Passion isn't intellectual or rational; it comes from the heart, and to fulfill it, you must express deeply held feelings. Passion implies desire, and if given a voice, your passion will inspire you to take action. Once you find your passion in life, you can't ignore it. Your purpose becomes compelling and creates an inner sense of urgency that makes you feel alive.

Over the past few years, so many people have said to me, "Sherry, I wish I had as much energy and enthusiasm as you do," or, "Sherry, you are so smart."

I tell each one of them the same thing: "I don't have anything that you don't have."

You see, we all have the same abilities and powers, it's just a matter of whether or not we believe in ourselves. I didn't grow up in a privileged environment. My parents weren't millionaires, and I started from the same humble beginnings as many of you did.

Each of us has our own path to follow in this world, and what is right for me may not be the correct direction for you. I have used my experiences to write a book to help others find their own path called Invent with Intent. SleekaVi© and the book, have been long-standing passions in my life that I'm honored to see come to fruition. They are only the first steps in my quest to help others achieve their dreams. You, on the other hand, may have a totally different mission. That's okay. Comparing ourselves to others stunts our growth; we need to find our own purpose in life and pursue it relentlessly. My husband, Ronny, and I learned a long time ago that money is only a vehicle—it can't buy happiness or love. Sure, it may be able to rent it for a while, but eventually the paint fades and the true colors begin to show. Unless you have a true purpose and passion for what you're doing, no amount of money can make it worthwhile. So, follow your heart and you will be rewarded both financially and spiritually.

Your life purpose should describe you perfectly. It should be invigorating and inspiring. Sometimes, your actual life or work history turns out to be completely different from your purpose. This is a very good indicator that you have been living the wrong life or working in the wrong occupation. Essentially, you've been living a life that doesn't fit you. If your life purpose and your actual history don't match, then, using your life purpose as the starting point, you might want to start planning a new, more fitting and rewarding life, career, or both.

It can be difficult to understand what it means to "be." We spend more of our time "doing" or "having." When you are "being," your vision of who you are can express itself. You will be drawn to your passion and inspire others to do the same. In the "having" mode, you feel driven but don't have a clear direction. You must have a clear vision of what you want in life, because without it, you will inevitably end up living according to someone else's vision for you. Without a plan in place, your purpose will never be revealed to you. Your vision represents what you want to focus on and what you want to accomplish in your life. Tapping into the divine power of your vision is the true essence of happiness, and true happiness spawns greatness in all areas of life. Success, to me, is being truly happy.

Shifting Your Mindset

THE LIMITATIONS WE place upon ourselves are about as realistic as the storyline in a musical—they are pure fiction. While we must accept the reality of the moment, we are not forever bound to it. The personal limitations you have accepted can be relinquished any time you wish. By persistently using your imagination, you can discard the old script and introduce a completely new story. To free yourself of all the misconceptions that are holding you back and have all that you truly desire, all you have to do is believe.

The power of imagination is one of the greatest forces in the universe. Human progress has developed in direct proportion to the collective imagination. Combining imagination with creativity gives us more than just mental images—it produces and brings about real things. I am reminded of this every time I look at my caddy. When we creatively imagine something, we actually cause it to come into being because it has been formed, for the first time, in our minds. This allows us to transform our lives through the power of creative imagination. Whatever idea you hold in your imagination, whether it is negative or positive, constructive or destructive, it will produce similar results in your life. When I first set out on this invention mission, I had no idea what was involved in actually filing a patent application and working with 3D draftsmen. I started visualizing a completed caddy and a very successful company, and those thoughts created daily opportunities for me. Because I was able to recognize these opportunities, I attained my goals at a rapid speed.

Creative imagination can be used to overcome disease and push the human body to exceptional feats. All problems are really opportunities in disguise, so we must examine every so-called crisis in our lives for the opportunity hidden within it. Our conscious mind often deceives us because it is dependent on the outside world. To free ourselves of the limitations of our conscious minds, we must shift our focus inward. To continue to look for inspiration externally is to continue to experience those conditions that have been holding us back.

You should be constantly running a mental movie with yourself as the star of the show. These images you create will determine your personal behavior and the kind of life you lead. Through your imagination, you have the power to mentally create a new life for yourself. If you can see yourself as achieving your desires, they will become reality. You are a self-fulfilling prophecy. What you are thinking about today is a clear indication of what you will be experiencing in the future.

Imagine yourself having and doing the things you want. Feel yourself enjoying them. See the details, colors, places, and people as vividly as you can. Hold these images clearly in your mind, and most importantly, put yourself in the picture.

Give thanks in advance. This may seem like a strange concept, especially if you don't understand the principle, but by giving thanks in advance, you are acknowledging that what you want is on its way to you. I start every day by giving thanks. When you begin doing this, conditions will start to change because you will be reaching for a higher dimension of consciousness. You will be in a state of magnetic attraction, unleashing your imagination and creativity.

Years ago, I studied the work of many of our great leaders. Once I began reading books and listening to audio books from these great teachers, I discovered a common thread in all of their stories. This common thread provided me an underlying truth to our existence. We really are all the same and how we perceive our lives and what we expect from life is what we get. Once I discovered this, I was set free. This knowledge has been the cause of my true happiness and has inspired me to move forward with my dreams. I only began to understand the mysteries of the universe in my forties, but I am finally happy. Looking back with regret doesn't do anybody any good. Walt Disney World employees urge us to "keep moving forward," and that is exactly what I do!

It is my intention to inspire everyone to follow their dreams. Each and every one of us is blessed with the same guidance mechanism, but we need to recognize it and move forward to achieve true success. Living a life you actually create is an indescribable feeling, and it's worth it!

Sherry Wilsher
Babe in Pink

About Sherry Wilsher:

SHERRY WILSHER'S innovative mindset has taken her to unparalleled success. Her foresight and vision led her to create one of the first cosmetic dental imaging businesses in Texas and conquer the real estate market in Houston Texas generating millions in revenue. Combining her vast knowledge and expertise in marketing and advertising, Sherry's entrepreneurial spirit led to the invention of the Sleeka Vi Caddy™ offering women around the globe a better and more efficient beauty storage option and essentials. Her first book, *Invent with Intent* chronicles Sherry's entrepreneurial journey while promoting her philosophy that great things can happen at any point in life. Through personal achievement and dedication, she strives to help others accomplish their goals and live a life they once thought unimaginable.

FULL NAME: Sherry Wilsher

COMPANY NAME: Sleeka Vi Int'l. LLC

WEBSITE: SherryWilsher.com

EMAIL: Sherry@SherryWilsher.com

BONUS GIFT:
FREE Chapter from my upcoming book,
Invent with Intent, Fastest Path to Million Dollar Ideas

Babe in White

CHAPTER 8

Clarissa (Riza)
Gatdula-Calingasan:
Babe in White

"I can do everything through
Him who gives me strength."
— Philippians 4:13

I magine a young girl wearing her mother's clothes to school. She isn't wearing them because they fit, but because she doesn't have enough clothes of her own. That was me. Most children would think this is embarrassing or sad, but I looked at it much differently. I considered my mother's clothes a blessing because they meant that I didn't have to wear the same outfit over and over again. Even though we didn't have much money, my parents reinforced the message that poverty was only a temporary situation and that nothing is permanent in this world. The examples they set taught me to stay strong and keep a positive attitude during any and all circumstances. They never said a negative word about life, taught me the real meaning of hope, and built my character.

As the first born in my family, I was expected to act as a role model for my siblings. Responsibility was the first word I learned. My parents exposed me to entrepreneurship and my mother taught me that with faith and the right mindset, success is possible for anyone. With the belief that opportunity is in your own hands, I pursued my university studies in Manila, Philippines, in the field of civil engineering. The entrepreneurial skills I learned from my parents were what got me through these years. I sold shirts and fruits, and had a summer job in a fast food restaurant to help support myself. Despite all the extra work, I excelled in my studies and graduated.

The Power of Action

FIFTEEN YEARS AGO, I noticed a family picture in a magazine and hoped that one day my life would look like that. I cut out the image and pasted it on my vision board. In 2004, my husband and I, along with our two children, immigrated to Manitoba, Canada. As I look back at the picture on my vision board, everyone is wearing winter clothes and much to my surprise, we moved to the coldest province in Canada. Consciously or unconsciously, every action you take will lead you toward your future, just like the action of cutting and pasting a picture took us to a better life. We now live in the Winter City—Winnipeg, Manitoba—and continue to have a smile in our hearts as we live the life that God desires for us.

As I recognized the significance of my situation in life, I learned to trust God and to believe that His gifts will allow me to move forward and look for a better future. I remember one time in particular, my husband and I only had fifteen cents left in our bank account, and our credit cards were all maxed out. We didn't complain and worry. Without any hesitation, falling back on my belief that opportunity is in our hands no matter the circumstances, we continued to search and take risks for opportunities to improve our family's life in Canada.

You have probably taken action many times your life without realizing the consequences. As I said earlier, your actions are conscious or unconscious decisions. The problem is that your actions can inhibit your success. What if I had never cut out that family's picture, and had lived believing that I would always live in poverty? You see, I didn't let my fifteen-cent story have a negative effect on me. I made the decision to take deliberate action to improve my life. That is the difference between a successful and an unsuccessful person. One takes deliberate action to better their life, while the other unconsciously acts by accepting their lot , not realizing the potential consequences. Imagine how much more you could achieve by taking positive action each day.

By focusing on your goals, believing that you can achieve them, and taking deliberate actions to make them happen, you will get the life you've always dreamed of. I never let my circumstances hinder the pursuit of my goals and dreams; instead, I followed the path of successful risk-taking entrepreneurs. You must take responsibility for the events in your life. We've all made promises that our lives will be different, but only those who take action will actually make a change.

Success is a process, not a one time event, and it requires taking both small and large actions over time. The best method of achieving success is by regularly setting goals. I always set impossible goals for myself. My present goal is to buy multiple properties with the profits from my travel business, and one of my biggest goals is to inspire people and teach them that anybody with a strong desire has the ability to succeed…through my Life and Business Coaching Programs.

I enjoy building my business because it doesn't feel like work to me. When you are doing something you're passionate about, even in tough times, you'll be focused on achieving your goals. Once you set your motivating goals, take action to move closer to them. Without action, you can't expect any significant changes in your life. It is also important to keep an open mind about any potential opportunities that come across your path. Remember, as you set goals you'll begin noticing many more avenues for accomplishing these goals because the scope of your attention expands. Always be open to new opportunities, and don't be afraid to take action. When you do take action, don't be afraid to change your course if something doesn't work out the way you expected it to. Sometimes, we must be willing to take detours to reach our ultimate destinations.

RISK

THE TERM RISK describes the probability of a future undesirable event as a result of a present decision. In life, we face risks all the time. Risk is, by nature, scary and unpredictable. We felt this way when we moved to Canada—we'd left for uncharted territory with no certainty of success. The rewards of our risk, however, were great. We have a wonderful life now and are helping others achieve the same level of success.

There were risks that we considered worth taking, and those that we avoided because they wouldn't help us gain anything. Even with a strong plan for your life, you will encounter some challenges from time to time. I embrace these challenges. I have created my own definition of RISK: Road to Influence your Success and Knowledge. It represents why I believe it is so important to take chances, and in this sense, I am a natural risk taker. My secret for taking RISKs is to determine specific actions that will produce results.

When I came to Canada, I took a risk. When I started in the network marketing business, I took a risk. I did all this with the knowledge that God had a plan for me and I was supposed to follow it with unwavering faith. I would have never taken these risks had I not believed and trusted in my Savior.

Sometimes I failed, but at least I took the risk. Life is void of meaning without faith and it is impossible to please God without it. To me, taking a risk amounts to having faith.

Now faith is the substance of things hoped for, the evidence of things not seen.
—Hebrews 11:1

Faith is one of the fundamental pillars of my life. People have different levels of faith, some big, some small. Sometimes bad things happen in life, and they can drain us of all faith and make it hard to believe that God is really there for us. These are the moments that test us to keep believing that God will deliver us from adversity. I know that I've been tested many times in my life, but I focused on what I wanted, had faith, and moved ahead with confidence. We must take each obstacle in our lives as an opportunity to increase our faith and to build our character.

It is inevitable that we will all face risks in life. Some will be easy to handle and some will be challenging. Faith will enable you to decide which risks to take and which ones to avoid. If we want to be successful, we have to face the risks that confront us with the knowledge that God is on our side and wants what's best for us. Whether you succeed or fail, taking risks will challenge you, reaffirm your faith in your strength and abilities, and give you the confidence to push yourself even further. The risks my family took when we left the Philippines are fond memories now, and I look forward to taking even bigger risks in the future.

Life doesn't come with guarantees. Every time I have to take a risk, I ask myself, "Why?" and soon, the "How?" falls into place. People who don't take risks rarely achieve what they want in life. Be brave and act with faith. Realize that you will never have enough information, research, knowledge, or experience to make perfect decisions, so take what you have and do the best that you can.

There is an old saying, "The greatest regret in our life is the risk that we didn't take." I am glad that I took the risk of becoming a Life and Business Coach and launching our successful online travel business.

Challenges and Blessings

THE HISTORY OF MY past became the indication of my future. I am a dreamer who is constantly tested and strengthened by challenges. When we moved to Canada, our situation changed dramatically. We were forced by circumstance to do different things than we might have preferred. Our lifestyles didn't change, so we lost our money. Despite our lack of money, I continued to take the risk of looking for the opportunities my new country had to offer. Opportunity after opportunity, challenge after challenge, debt after debt—we found our faith. We saw then, and still do, the promise of God, which led us to the opportunities that created all that we have now.

We needed to start earning money as soon as we arrived in Canada, since I wasn't able to practice my profession, civil engineering. As I looked for work, I was exposed to many successful people who led me to a new career in the network marketing industry. It was a challenge and a risk, but I decided to take action and fully commit to building a business that I thought would change me and my family's life.

Some people laughed at my dreams and told me I'd never be able to achieve them. In my family, however, we have always had big dreams and no one was going to tell us otherwise. My enthusiasm for my hopes and dreams sometimes turned people off, because they hadn't seen any changes in our lifestyle since we'd arrived in Canada three years earlier. I, however, understood the Law of Gender, which states that every seed has a gestation period and that ideas are spiritual seeds that will, when the time is right, become physical results. Your goals will become reality in perfect time—in His time. I knew this to be true, so I held on to my dreams, hoped for the best, and with faith and actions my challenges soon became my blessings.

Along my journey, I worked with people who were desperate to get all the credit and money they could, even if they needed to behave in an unethical way. I couldn't live like this and chose to take the ethical path while those around me acted in unscrupulous ways. Even though we had no money, I felt blessed—I would rather be broke and have my values, than be rich and live among unethical people. This painful experience taught me how to be a stronger person, and every time I think back to this time, I'm reminded of Wayne Dyer's quote, "Try viewing everyone who comes into your life as a teacher."

I used these memories to help me move forward and build a travel business. I didn't have any experience in this field, but I was passionate about the beauty of God's creations in this world, and this passion inspired me to succeed. I was no stranger to the idea that a successful business takes time to grow. I strategically developed my skills and treated my new online travel business the same way I'd treated all of my previous businesses endeavors, with 100% commitment and dedication to make it work.

I had successful leaders mentor me and, in less than a year, without experience or knowledge about the industry, I'd set records that inspired many other entrepreneurs. I met various interesting network marketers, and I fell in love with time and money leveraging concepts. In spite of the challenges I faced and the skepticism of the people around me, I achieved my goals. Even though people tried to pull me down, I strengthened my character, and despite the economic crisis, I achieved my dreams and have helped countless people realize their dreams as well.

Partnered with my husband and the faith that God gave us, I operate my dream travel business. Our success has allowed us to do more, have more, and be more, and has inspired many people to turbo-charge their journey to wealth by taking advantage of network marketing. Although we still face challenges, our faith is stronger, our dreams are bigger, our happiness became joy, our richness became wealth, and our house became home—a home heated by love, fuelled by faith, and structured by dreams.

I achieved my impossible dreams, and so can you. The blessing of having a unique travel business turned our lives around. My business offers people a product they want; it has a great support system and a hybrid marketing plan; and is in line with the way people want to use the internet today. I am committed to empowering people and connecting them to opportunities through spiritual awareness. I am very passionate about inspiring people and teaching them that our journey is designed to discover the magic of winning!

I live by the principle that whatever you focus on expands. Focus on your business, and your business will expand. Focus on good health, and your good health will expand. Focus on what you want, and you will create it. I'm privileged to be able to share my journey with you and I hope that it encourages you to move forward and make a difference in your own life. Remember that success is a mindset and use your fear to inspire you with the courage to live the life designed for you by our Creator. Take action and discover the winner inside you. The future is in your hands, the moment is in your words, the reality is in your thinking, and the truth is within you. Your actions will guide you toward the promise made to you by our Creator.

Clarissa "Riza"
Gatdula-Calingasan
Babe in White

About Clarissa "Riza" Gatdula-Calingasan:

CLARISSA GATDULA-CALINGASAN is the founder of Empowerment MindStyle Coaching Centre. As a Life and Business Coach, she combines weight management, business and life skills programs with her MindStyle coaching. Clarissa shares her passion for health and wellness through her Multidimensional Weight Management Program. Along with her Coaching Centre, Carissa operates an online travel business. She offers her clients wholesale prices, convenience, and gives them five star service. As an entrepreneur, investor, speaker, author, motivator, coach, and Civil Engineer, she is dedicated to touch people's lives around the world and committed to take them from the brink of possibility to the path of infinite probability.

FULL NAME: Clarissa "Riza" Gatdula-Calingasan

COMPANY NAME: Jayriz Partners

WEBSITE: www.traveltoearn.com

EMAIL: jayriz_travel@yahoo.com

BONUS GIFT: Free Business. Limited Time Offer!

Babe in White

Babe in Pinstripe

CHAPTER 9

Sally Walker:
Babe in Pinstripe

"Never say quit."

As a child, I always felt a little different. I was raised to be independent and I've carried this trait throughout my life. Unlike the other children, I knew what I wanted to do with my life at a very early age; however, life dealt me a severe blow at the age of thirteen. My father died, leaving me alone with a mother who was probably less independent than I was at that point. I have memories of being the stronger person in the home, and for the first time, my life as I knew it changed dramatically.

My older brother had already left home when my father died, so I was left alone with many new responsibilities. At grammar school, I excelled in athletics, I was captain of the netball and hockey teams, and I was enthusiastic about science, especially human biology. My passion for understanding the body and its inner workings was already developing.

My relationship with my mother became more sisterly than mother-daughter. After she remarried, we returned to a more traditional mother-daughter relationship, but one that became increasingly detached as her attention focused more on her husband and her new life. As the years passed, my sense of independence helped me continue to plan for my future and work toward my goals. In 1975, my mother informed me that she was packing up my childhood home to move with her new husband to Scotland—for the second time in my life, an external force would change my world. I was eighteen at the time, and I knew that from that point on, I would have to be responsible for my own happiness and success. I moved to Denmark in 1979, and two years later, I met the man I thought I was going to spend the rest of my life with. The following September, we were married. His business was demanding, so I quit my work as a physiotherapist to assist him, and in doing so, gave up my purpose to be a part of his dream.

My husband liked to have his business associates and customers dine in our home and stay with us rather than at hotels, so I spent the majority of my days being the consummate innkeeper. When I wasn't playing hostess, he and I traveled around the world for his business. For seven years, I lived a busy, challenging, exciting life supporting him and his company. The luxurious lifestyle I had become accustomed to came to an abrupt end when my husband was imprisoned; as a result, we divorced. My world as I knew it collapsed, and yet again, I needed to rise out of the ashes of my former life and find a way to support myself. It was time to realign myself with my purpose.

I couldn't find a job, so I created my own. Finding myself again was challenging, but I knew deep inside that I was capable of anything and worked diligently to rebuild my life. Despite having lost focus during my marriage, I have no regrets, because during those seven years I had so many wonderful experiences and I learned a great deal. Now, however, I have to create my own excitement in life and live on my own terms, and I'm thankful for those experiences because they help me with my present-day challenges.

After almost two decades working with my passion—initially in the realm of traditional physiotherapy and later to live my purpose more effectively—I expanded my areas of expertise into other fields. Now, every day is a blessing, because I work and live in the world I dared to create for myself.

You Only Live Once, So Make It On Purpose

I'VE KNOWN I wanted to be a physiotherapist from the age of fourteen. Even though I was told repeatedly that my grades weren't good enough, I didn't give up on my dream. I knew it was part of my purpose. Each one of us is born with a purpose, though most of us don't realize it until adulthood, and some never do. Unfortunately, many people don't find their purpose until they've endured many years of trial and error that eventually lead to self-discovery. These people go through life taking jobs to cover financial needs or living according to someone else's wishes. My childhood forced me to grow up quickly, and I was fortunate enough to realize my purpose at an early age. The truth of the matter is that it doesn't have to take years to find your purpose. All you need to do is focus on you.

Sit yourself down in a quiet room and write a list of what you're good at, what you love to do, what gives you the most pleasure, and what your gifts, talents, and interests are. Writing this list is the first step toward realizing your purpose. You see, your purpose is what drives you; some people say it's your "why."

We are each put in this universe for a specific purpose, to do something extraordinary. You are doing a grave disservice to yourself and to others if you don't discover and live out your purpose in life. My purpose is to inform, inspire, and support people from all over the world to take more responsibility for their body and their life. I do this every day in so many ways, and I love it. This is my "why."

It is why my working day begins at 6:45 a.m., with fifteen to twenty minutes of exercise followed by a shower and a breakfast smoothie of raw eggs, fruit, nuts, oil, and water. It is why, on clinic days, I consult and coach clients in person, over the phone, or online, sometimes individually, and other times in groups. It is why, on non-clinic days, I use my time to prepare lectures and write books or articles. It is also why every day is a working day for me. Now, for some of you reading this, working every day might sound unappealing, not to mention the raw eggs for breakfast. But for me, work is not a chore. It is my "why," my passion, my hobby, my purpose, and when you're working on purpose, you are living your life to the fullest. Of course, I also have time off, because my other passion is my partner and he can be very time consuming!

Every day, I help people meet their physical, emotional, and mental health goals. Where would they be if I ignored my calling in life? I know they benefit from my services because I see the expressions of enlightenment on their faces when I give one of my talks, not to mention the feelings of gratitude my pupils express when they have made the necessary changes and achieved their desired results.

Far too often, people just don't believe in themselves, which impedes their path to finding and living their purpose. I believed in myself enough to excel in my studies, finish school with high merits, and move to a country where I didn't even speak the language! I knew nothing of Denmark and the language was a nightmare to learn. I spent my first nights dreaming of this rather ugly language, the foreign sounds flying around my head, unable to make out where one word ended and the next started. With a steadfast belief in myself, I learned to speak and write Danish and today I am fluent.

Imagine what my family and friends thought about me moving to a country where I didn't even know the language. I didn't listen to their doubts, and I didn't let them influence me in any way. I started my new life in the south of Denmark, in a small town called Sønderborg, which I quickly outgrew. I soon made my way to wonderful Copenhagen, where I worked at Rigshospital, the city's main hospital. Most people thought it was quite a big step for a twenty-two-year-old girl to give up her life in the U.K., pack her bags and move to a strange, cold country where she didn't even speak the language, but I was an expert in starting over, having already done it twice. For me, this was not the biggest challenge of my life and I believed that I could do it.

You have to believe in yourself and listen your inner voice above all else. It will never steer you in the wrong direction. Our family and friends don't share our purpose and, for one reason or another, may try to discourage us from following life's calling. As I mentioned earlier, I was young when I realized my purpose, and I was secretive because I didn't want to hear any negative feedback. At that point in my life my family had their own agenda, which didn't necessarily always have my best interests at heart. I'm not telling you to keep secrets from your family and friends, but I do suggest that you filter their words and limit the effect they can have on you and your beliefs.

Although friends and family usually mean well with their advice, it can prevent you from finding your purpose in life. Remember that their advice is based on what they believe is possible. You must ask yourself what you believe is possible. Many people fear change and therefore don't want anyone around them to change. I know it may seem difficult, but separating yourself from those who don't have your best interests at heart will be in your own best interest. I would encourage you to spend less time with people who always bring you down, or invite them to change their attitudes and join your journey. Build yourself a social network full of people who think like you and who can offer support, encouragement, and guidance in your quest.

You will find that everyone has a different story to tell and their own special strategy. Seek out people who have already accomplished goals similar to yours and let them inspire you, for they know "how." Your task is to find your "why"—let others help you with the "how" and you can avoid making big mistakes.

I believe that if you live your life doing what you're meant to do, tremendous good fortune will follow. Good fortune can take the shape of money, but it can also come to you as peace, balance, and fulfillment. The feelings of gratitude bestowed upon you when you help another person by using your natural talents are immeasurable. These are the gifts that cause you to enjoy your life, not the amount of money you earn. Just think of how many people make heaps of money, but are still miserable. Your purpose defines, describes, inspires, and guides you through life. True success in life begins with your purpose.

Think and Grow Rich

UNKNOWINGLY, I'VE BEEN using principles from *Think and Grow Rich* my whole life, particularly those having to do with faith. Deep inside, I never doubt my belief or my purpose. On the surface, I occasionally question my abilities, but whenever tested, I never say quit knowing in my heart that I am able. Thus, on a subconscious level my faith in myself is unwavering. Faith is an amazing phenomenon, but how can something so powerful be invisible? I like to compare faith to oxygen. Red blood cells carry oxygen from our lungs to every single cell in our bodies. Oxygen is necessary for our survival and quality of life. If your oxygen levels are low, your quality of life is poor, and the same applies to faith. Without faith, you lack meaning in your life. To me, faith is no different from oxygen. You can feel faith working and guiding you, but like oxygen, it is invisible. Only the effects of its presence prove its existence.

Many times throughout my life, my faith has been a beacon to guide me. When I took a momentous leap and left the financial security of traditional physiotherapy to open my own private clinic, I was scared and excited at the same time. My faith, however, enabled me to overcome my fears and believe in myself. I secured contracts with many companies to provide on-site health services, including massage, physiotherapy, exercise, nutritional advice, and stress coaching, and I got so busy I had to hire additional therapists. If I hadn't had the faith to pursue my dreams, I wouldn't have had the power to reeducate myself in the areas of kinesiology, acupuncture, nutrition, stress, and the mind. The strength of our faith affects the way we perceive the value of our abilities. If we believe in our capabilities, we believe that we can accomplish whatever we set our minds to.

To have faith, you must also believe. The power of faith is relative to your belief that something is possible. I've survived two financial crises and the media tells me I am in the middle of a third, but my faith doesn't allow me to focus on this. Instead, it gives me the courage to be creative and look for solutions. Being tuned in to the challenges that surround you is a good thing; it gets your adrenaline pumping a little harder and pushes you to find a solution. When you truly believe you can do something, your mind will find a way to accomplish it. Remember that your belief is embedded in the core of your being. You can accomplish any goal with faith, just like I did. Never let someone tell you that you can't do something, and never doubt yourself for a minute.

One of the reasons so many women lack faith is because they have no patience. In a society obsessed with instant gratification, we don't like to wait for anything. Technology affords us this luxury— if you want a song, just download it. While computers, iPhones, and Blackberrys seem to be able to give us whatever we want when we want it, they can't give us patience. Patience is an important quality to possess, because it allows us to endure seemingly eternal waits and delays. Patience also helps us to remain calm in the face of adversity. It has never been easy to be patient, but in today's world, it is harder than ever.

Everyone wants to multitask and accomplish as much as possible as soon as possible, only to accomplish even more. Hurry, hurry, hurry. What's the point? No matter how fast you run, success won't happen overnight. I once heard someone say that they were a twenty-year overnight success. With patience, you can cultivate and nurture your optimal success. Remind yourself often that success takes time, and that there will always be situations, circumstances, and events that frustrate and annoy you. You can't change them—you can only change you. Accept obstacles and challenges with the understanding that they happened for a reason and soon, with patience, you'll know why.

With faith and patience, I worked at a fitness center for seven years until I opened my own clinic. Even though I knew I would eventually open my own clinic, one other attribute helped get me through those years: persistence. Persistence allows you to succeed in life, no matter what obstacles you encounter.

Persistence can be difficult. There are mornings where you wake up and just want to stay in bed all day. It is during times like these that our persistence has to shine through and make us do what we'd rather avoid. Persistence gives us the determination to keep going, no matter the odds. Whenever I encountered an obstacle in my life, I faced it knowing that I would persist through the challenge. We have the ability to surprise ourselves, and often times, you'll discover that you're able to do things that you didn't think were possible.

When you face a new challenge with a persistent attitude and an eagerness to succeed, chances are you will. Many of us know what we need to do, yet we don't do it. No instant fix or get rich quick scheme can take the place of persistence—it is a skill you need to master. With faith, patience, and persistence, you will achieve success in everything you do. As Napoleon Hill said, "Riches do not respond to wishes. They respond only to definite plans, backed by definite desires, through constant persistence."

Can you remember a time in your life when you wanted something so much you didn't give up until you got it? You need to find this feeling of determination and hold on to it, through thick and thin, when you set your goal. Remember, if you set your goal based on your purpose, you are going to be doing things that feel right.

Progress before Perfection

WE ALL HAVE the potential to accomplish our goals in life, but finding a mentor can speed up the process. Find other people who have already succeeded in your chosen field. Learn how they became so successful, mimic their actions, and once you attain your goals, turn back and show others how to achieve the same success.

Along with the ability to help you achieve success in life, mentors have many more qualities to offer you. They can provide you with guidance and dramatically shorten your learning curve by exposing you to their experiences, knowledge, mistakes, and triumphs. This much-needed advice and support encourages you to set goals and stay focused. Your mentor will be one of your closet allies, and you'll rely on them when faced with overwhelming obstacles, and run to them to celebrate your well-deserved successes. Finding a mentor will not only secure your success and help you accomplish your goals, it will also give you a great sense of achievement when you make your mentor proud.

Every time you start a new endeavor, there is a good deal to learn, and this can often seem overwhelming. You can't succeed at everything, so don't give up, remain focused, ask yourself what you can learn from your mistakes, and consult with your mentor. With a mentor, you can see concepts in motion, then emulate their techniques, and finally, tailor them to fit your personality and business. Many of the greatest minds in history, Albert Einstein, Thomas Edison, Bill Gates, had mentors who guided them on their paths to success.

It is important to find a mentor who is successful in your chosen career field. One of best arenas for finding such a person is within professional associations or civic groups. Joining these types of organizations exposes you to a variety of individuals and to various experiences. Networking is imperative for success, because the more people you know in your profession, the better your chances for growth and opportunity. Attend local meetings, seminars, and presentations in your field.

Participating in these types of activities gives you valuable knowledge and helps you find people who are willing to take you under their wing and help you work toward your own success. Attend and sign up for training, professional development courses, and newsletters. All of these activities will help you forge your path to success. When you are an active and visible participant, people will notice your dedication, and will likely provide you with opportunities that you would have otherwise missed.

To achieve any amount of success in life, you must set goals for yourself. I've always set goals, and I've met or exceeded every single one. My present goal is to be a renowned author and speaker in the field of health and wellness, and to do this I believe I'll have to spend less time with individual clients. Once again, I am moving out of my comfort zone, but I believe my message is very important for people today, and my goal is to get my message and experiences out to a larger forum. Another goal of mine is to sell e-books and e-courses from my website, www.sallywalker.com. I know in my heart that I will succeed.

Pick goals that challenge you professionally, mentally, and even spiritually. Make investments that stretch your abilities and require high levels of creativity and energy to conquer. Remember to get the adrenaline pumping and to continuously challenge yourself. Goals that don't challenge you move you sideways, not forward. You need to get out of your comfort zone and force yourself to learn new and difficult skills. When I moved to a country and didn't even know the language, I was way out of my comfort zone, and it was one of the greatest decisions I ever made!

Surround yourself with like-minded people who see challenges as possibilities instead of obstacles and problems; people who say yes more than they say no. Even if it hurts, listen to your inner voice—it will end up hurting much more later if you ignore it. Visualize yourself in possession of what you want, celebrate small victories along the way, and enjoy the journey, because once you reach your goal, it's time to set a new goal and start again.

Because I set and achieve goals regularly, my life is always full and exciting. I travel frequently to various countries to educate myself so that I can always provide my clients with the newest knowledge and perspectives. My time and my life are my own, and I am the reason for my success and my failures. When times are good, I have only myself to thank, and when they are bad, I have only myself to blame, and being accountable for my actions gives me a deep sense satisfaction.

My life has presented its fair share of challenges, but has also been fulfilling in so many ways, and I am sure it will continue this way—when you stick your neck out, sometimes your head gets hit. Today, I am working on my own terms and for me, this is the ultimate dream. Actions speak louder than words, so when you need to take action, "just do it." You don't need to know the way, just take the first step. Listen to your inner voice, believe in yourself, and have faith. Sometimes things don't go exactly as planned, but don't take it personally. If you're living according to your purpose and acting with faith, patience, and persistence, you'll achieve every success life has in store for you. Looking back on my life, I wouldn't change one single action I took. Every mistake holds a message, and I am where I am today because of my experiences and the lessons my mistakes have taught me. Remember, the perfect moment is now, so with faith, patience, and persistence, "just do it."

Sally Walker
Babe in Pinstripe

About Sally Walker:

SALLY WALKER is a physiotherapist who specializes in kinesiology, acupuncture, nutrition, stress, and the mind. Her experience as a physiotherapist spans the globe where she has worked with the Danish National Tennis Team and the Hotel Oriental in Hong Kong. In 2005, she returned to Copenhagen to open the Goodlife Clinic where she and her team of 10 specialized therapists worked together holistically to bring physical, mental and emotional well being to her clients. In 2008, Sally and two colleagues established BodyMindBuilding which focuses on healthy habits and weight loss through intensive weekend courses, cooking courses, group coaching and seminars as well as an education system for consultants wanting to help others.

FULL NAME: Sally Walker

COMPANY NAME: Sally Walker

WEBSITE: www.sallywalkers.com

EMAIL: sally@sallywalkers.com

BONUS GIFT: Analysis of Goodlife Wheel

Babe in Red

CHAPTER 10

Dr. Cynthia Barnett:
Babe in Red

*"With God by my side as my designer
success is guaranteed as the mosaic of
my life unfolds."*

Oprah is one of my greatest inspirations. We are both on a mission to teach women that they can be and do anything they want in order to regain control of their lives, and that they can be happier, more fulfilled, and have a more meaningful life. I want to share my life story and inspire people with my struggle to overcome challenges and attain the life of my dreams. Looking at my life today, it's hard to believe that this petite, self-assured, successful woman is the same young girl who arrived in the United States forty years earlier with no money. Who could imagine that this successful woman once had to search for coins to take the train home to the Bronx, where she lived in a one-bedroom apartment with her mother, stepfather, and a two-year-old brother?

Reading this, you may think, "Wow, she came to this country with nothing," but that's not true. I came to this country with a dream. I wanted to get the best education that this country had to offer, even though I had no money, no resources, and no guidance. I did have the desire, and I was willing to do whatever it would take to achieve my dream. Many obstacles stood in my way, and even when I felt overwhelmed, I always saw the light at the end of that tunnel and kept the vision alive.

After many years, I found myself to be a single mother with three children, and living on a small budget. But this did little to squelch my burning desire to earn the highest degree colleges offered in my field. My dream was an obsession, and I worked any job I could find to get myself through college. I worked in a pen factory inserting the ink into ballpoint pens, I cleaned houses, I filed documents for an insurance company, and I waited tables in a convalescent home, but I always knew I was working toward my goal.

After a thirty-year career in public education as a teacher, a counselor, and an assistant principal in high school, I decided to "refire" my life, instead of "retire" it, so I left the schoolhouse to become an entrepreneur. Forming my own organization was an education in itself. I had so much to learn, and my education continues today as I learn new business skills by taking classes— and I still make mistakes! I know I have a lot to learn as I work to build a lasting business, because the learning process is ongoing. One of the most rewarding parts of my business is hearing people tell me that I helped empower them to take control of their lives, make changes, and start to achieve their dreams and live a happier, more fulfilled, and meaningful life.

I Will Survive

MY DIVORCE STANDS out in my mind as one of worst stumbling blocks in my life. During my marriage, I was overweight, had no self-esteem, and very little self-worth. Going through my divorce, I thought that my feelings of hopelessness and sadness would never end. I know the power of determination and persistence carried me through those extremely difficult and exhausting months. Believe me, I often felt discouraged and wanted to give up. As I look back over the past twenty-five years, I'm grateful I used the innate power of persistence that we all have inside of us.

My worst nightmare happened right before my eyes, and I never saw it coming. My self-esteem, which was already fragile, crumbled. My heart was shattered, my very being was shaken, and I was devastated. My perfect family was unraveling thread by thread and there was nothing I could do to stop it. My children were losing a father whom I desperately wanted for them, and I was being left alone.

I remember the scene like it happened yesterday. On a Sunday morning, my husband called me into the family room and told me he wanted a divorce. I couldn't believe it! He wanted to destroy our family. How could he? What kind of bastard was he? I knew we'd been going through a rough patch, but I never imagined he wanted to leave. Every emotion tumbled over me: fear, failure, doubt. I pleaded to go to marriage counseling. I begged him to reconsider. All I could see was that I was going to be left alone to raise three children with no father.. My future seemed to consist of loneliness, fatherless children, and broken dreams.

I begged my husband not to leave me, I pleaded for my life, my dreams, and my sanity. I was willing to accept any crumbs he might offer, but it was to no avail. I humiliated myself further by promising to lose more weight. You see, I was heavy and I foolishly thought that that was his reason for leaving. After all, his lover was thin.

No matter what I said or promised, he was determined to leave. He refused to admit that it was because of the affair he'd been having with my so-called friend. Rather, he said, he wasn't in love with me anymore and needed to live on his own. That beautiful Sunday morning, I watched him pack his clothes and leave. The pain was so bad I could hardly bear it. I needed some time, so I went for a walk and cried all the way to the beach. After all these years, I can still recall the intensity of that morning.

After my return from the beach that Sunday morning, I was left to care for three children, a three, five, and ten-year-old. My oldest daughter understood what was happening, but the two little ones didn't. He promised to support them, but true to his character, he showed the same irresponsibility to his children as he did to our marriage. At first, he made a few attempts to see the children, but although he lived less than an hour away, the weeks became months and the months became years between visits.

Still, I allowed him to see the children whenever he wanted, despite the fact that he didn't support them. The only real money I ever got from him was during a brief period when his salary was being garnished. Other than that, a judge once put him in prison and wouldn't allow his release until he paid me $1,000. A friend of his gave him the money by the end of the day, and that was the last support we received from him for the next twenty years.

I had two choices. I could allow myself to drown, or force myself to swim. Dusting off the sorrow and wiping away my tears, I went to work. This was the primary turning point in my life. I prayed and continued to attend the weight support group I'd been a member of for two years. At my job, I was making $18,000 a year—not nearly enough to support three children, take care of a house, and handle everything else necessary for survival. During the first year on my own, I had to replace the roof and the septic tank, and many times, I didn't have any oil to heat the house. I considered selling the house but quickly quashed that idea—my children needed stability after their father had walked out on them, and uprooting them would be too traumatic. Instead, I took a summer job teaching macramé in adult education centers to make ends meet. In the meantime, I discovered every consignment store and tag sale in the area to clothe my children.

I will never forget the friend who gave us her daughter's clothes, or the friend who put oil in our heating tank one winter. I am eternally grateful to the friend who lent me her car until I could afford to buy one, and to the friend who paid my car insurance so I could drive to work. My husband's family never offered a hand, and I never asked for their help. I didn't ask my family members for help either; they had their own problems and struggles. I found out what I needed to do every step of the way, and I did it. I became handy around the house, although getting to that point involved making a lot of mistakes along the way. I painted, did the plumbing, did carpentry work, and cut the grass. If any upkeep or maintenance needed to be done, I did it. I don't know how I did it, I only knew that I intended to survive. Gloria Gaynor's song, I Will Survive, became my theme and my anchor.

I worried whether I'd ever find a new partner who would want to be with my three children and me. Well, it happened. I found someone who cared for me because I was special. He liked my independence and determination. Before long, I decided to go back to school because, in the education field, more degrees mean more money. I also knew I liked variety and that I didn't want to be an elementary teacher forever. I found a babysitter for the children and earned a Master's degree in counseling and, later, a doctorate in administration from Columbia University. In the meantime, my daughters grew up beautifully. My dreams for them came true when they all graduated from college and today, at the ages of thirty-six, thirty-two, and twenty-nine, they have developed into independent women.

As horrific as my divorce was at the time, it marked the end of having a husband who hadn't worked for two years, and refused to take a job to support his family. I couldn't see that at the time. After all, I had just been mortified, humiliated, and jilted by a man who didn't love me, and I couldn't do anything about it. I had been ready to settle for crumbs from a man who was unavailable to me, who had several affairs over the course of our twelve-year marriage, who disappeared for days at a time and didn't tell me where he was, and who pretended he wanted what I wanted. In retrospect, my divorce marked the beginning of a journey toward survival, growth, self-sufficiency, and ultimately, happiness.

Taking a Stand

ONE OF MY ambitions had been to become an administrator at the local high school. My credentials were excellent—I had fifteen years of teaching experience, five years as a guidance counselor, and a doctorate degree from Columbia University. I was ready! When the opportunity arose, I applied for the position and felt confident that my interview went well. Two weeks later, I heard from another source—not the superintendent who interviewed me—that I didn't get the job. Imagine my disappointment when I heard who had landed the job: a white male whose credentials were far inferior to mine.

I felt betrayed by the superintendent who, five years earlier, had assured me that in a few years, they would need people with my energy and creativity for administrative positions. In fact, he was the one who had encouraged me to seek my administrative degree. Previously, I had applied for several positions at the elementary level, but my lack of administrative experience disqualified me from those positions. I could accept that because the people who got the positions had more experience than I did. In this case, the position didn't require previous experience, and I had all the necessary credentials.

I felt that I was being denied an opportunity that I deserved. Considering the injustice, unfairness, and obvious difference in credentials between me and the other applicant, I couldn't help but wonder if my race and gender were factors. I decided to find out about my legal rights. I consulted an attorney who specialized in discrimination. After I told him all the details, he assured me that he had never seen such a blatant case of discrimination. I knew I had to take a stand and file a lawsuit against the board of education and the superintendent. Needless to say, I was scared and frightened. I had never done anything like that before.

My attorney wrote to the superintendent, informing him of our intention to pursue the matter further if the injustice wasn't corrected. The letter read, "From everything I am able to discern in the course of my investigation of this matter, Dr. Barnett is a victim of racial and gender discrimination, and the action of the Board of Education is in clear violation of both federal and state discrimination laws."

After four weeks and several consultations with my attorney and the superintendent, I was offered the position of assistant principal at a middle school. I didn't accept the job, because it wasn't the position for which I had applied. A few days later, I received a call telling me to report to work at the high school to which I had applied. I was elated that I had won the fight, but I knew there was more agony to come. After all, by going into a school where I wasn't wanted, I was walking into a hornet's nest. The principal didn't want me there, nor did the other assistants, and the secretaries considered me a militant. In fact, it was worse than I imagined. I felt like the leaders in the civil rights days who had to break down walls to get justice, but this was 1992. I remember praying, "God, you walk in front of me and I will walk behind you."

My first day on the job, the principal gave me my assignments and that was it—no explanations, no showing me around the school, nothing! I didn't expect a warm welcome, but I was shocked at this ice-cold reception. I soon realized that the principal had set me up for failure by assigning me two-thirds of all the responsibilities, a heavier load than the other two experienced assistants carried combined. I looked at it analytically, and then broke down the many duties into bite-sized pieces.

The only people who welcomed me were the custodians. They supported me because they were proud that I had fought for the position. I was also blessed with a great secretary who became my friend and right-hand person. Her support and encouragement kept me going in those early days. During this time, I prayed a great deal and began a serious spiritual journey, concentrating on my personal growth. I knew I needed to be strong to survive in this negative atmosphere. I read *Dale Carnegie's How to Win Friends and Influence People,* and then took the Carnegie course.

Practicing the strategies I learned on the principal who didn't want me, I was determined to earn his respect the Dale Carnegie way. He was my evaluator and I did not want him to give me a negative evaluation. In Malcolm X's words, I intended to succeed "by any means necessary." Not only did I practice Dale Carnegie's strategies, I actually elicited my principal's evaluation every month, then followed up with a written summary of each meeting and what I planned to do with his suggestions for improvement. After three years of these monthly meetings for three years, I never got a negative evaluation from him. In fact, I believe he came to respect my work.

By persistently working on my personal growth over the ten years I spent in that position, I became a woman who had gained great strength and confidence; I felt I could do anything. When people ask me how I survived that time in my life, I say, "With a strong spiritual foundation and by putting God in the driver's seat, a person can do anything."

Persistence is Key

SUCCESS NEVER CAME easily to me—I had to work every step of the way. I struggled to get into college, and when I auditioned for music school, I was told that my skills weren't up to standard. Not ready to give up, I asked what I needed to do to gain admittance. I was told to hire a teacher and practice. I did, and I was accepted. While working on my doctorate degree, I had to retake the certification examination. The failures I've experienced have not deterred me. Instead, I've used them as lessons to get to the next step. All of these experiences have made me stronger and more confident.

Through persistence, hard work, and constant personal development, I achieved my dream of earning the highest degree in my career field—a doctorate in leadership from Columbia University—and of putting all three of my daughters through college. Today, my first daughter is an attorney, my second daughter a freelance surface design artist, and my third daughter is a teacher.

Everything I have done in life has prepared me for the work I am doing now. My skills as a teacher have prepared me to be a master facilitator, my skills as a counselor have helped me understand and have compassion for others, and my skills as a school administrator have helped me be a leader who knows how to delegate the items I am not good at so that I can focus on my strengths. Now that I've "retired" from the school system, I've "refired" my life as an entrepreneur with a passion for helping other women turn their dreams into reality. I am confident that my experiences will prove to be valuable resources for you. The strategies I used worked for me and have been working for all the people I've met through coaching, workshops, retreats, and keynote speeches.

Success happens when we take full control and make conscious choices that direct the course of our lives. We must live a spiritually focused life of passion, and learn to balance knowing who we are and living authentically. I assure you that no matter what obstacles you face, you have the inborn strength to overcome them and fulfill your dreams. With the help of God, you can do, have, and be anything you want. I have come a long, long way from the murky days that followed my divorce. I hope my story of struggle, fortitude, courage, and determination empowers you to never, ever give up. My inner strength is not unique—you, too, have the strength and courage to survive any obstacles in your life's path.

Dr. Cynthia Barnett
Babe in Red

About Dr. Cynthia Barnett:

With a B.Sc. from New York University, and an M.A. and Doctorate from Columbia University, Dr. Cynthia Barnett, a former Assistant High School Principal, retired to "re-fire" her life. A leading authority on how to reinvent yourself, she has been featured in Time Magazine, US News, and World Report as well as local newspapers and various television shows. As the author of Stop Singing the Blues, Prime Time Makeover and a Certified Facilitator of Stephen Covey's material, as well as a trained self esteem facilitator by Jack Canfield; she has made it her mission in life to teach people how to create meaningful and more fulfilled lives.

FULL NAME: Dr. Cynthia Barnett

COMPANY NAME: Peak Performance Solutions

WEBSITE: www.freestyleretreats.com

EMAIL: drcynthia@freestyleretreats.com

BONUS GIFT:
One hour of personal leadership coaching

Babe in Purple

CHAPTER 11

Lene Hansson:
Babe in Purple

*"I believe that it is not what happens
to you, it is the way you choose to
think about what happens, that
decides whether or not it is a good
or bad thing."*

— Lene Hansson

For many years, I suffered from allergies, asthma, hay fever, irritable bowel syndrome, and low energy. I tried diets from all over the world to lose weight and get rid of my illnesses, but nothing ever worked. I never felt any better than before, and sometimes I felt even worse. One day, I discovered the book *Fit for Life,* by Harvey and Marilyn Diamond, and my entire lifestyle changed. Not only did I feel great, I began writing books about nutrition and was able to work from home and spend more time with my son.

I believe love is the best medicine, so I raised my son the same way my mother raised me—with love and understanding. Our children are our responsibility, and they deserve to live rich lives full of laughter, activity and joy. They deserve to look in the mirror and be proud of who they are. This isn't about vanity; it's about self-confidence. If we don't provide our children with a foundation of healthy skills and habits, they will pay the consequences later in life. Today, my son is very balanced, and to see him happy is the best reward I can ever have.

When he was in kindergarten, I would pick him up every day at 2:00 p.m. so that we could be together. When he went to bed at night, I would work some more. I always adjusted my work schedule around his needs. Today, many business people make their career their first priority and their children come second. I have always disagreed with this attitude, so I made my son the most important part of my life. I started my business by writing books about nutrition from home. Seventeen years later, I'm still working, I'm enjoying every minute of it, and I'm currently educating myself in the field of homeopathy.

Follow Your Dreams

MY FATHER WAS always disappointed that I didn't go to university. Throughout my life, he's given me countless pieces of advice, none of which I agreed with. I chose to follow my dreams and do what I wanted to do. Finally, last year, he said to me, "Lene, I am so happy that you never listened to me and did what you believed in!" Instead of following his dream for me, I chose to follow my own, and now I've helped thousands of people live their lives without illness and obesity.

Many of us don't believe in our abilities, but if you don't believe in yourself, how can you follow your dreams? Before you can achieve your dreams, you have to get a true picture of yourself and what you are capable of. With a positive dream and a strong sense of belief, you can do anything you set your mind to do!

It's vital that you trust yourself and your abilities. Without self-confidence, people lack the ability to trust themselves and their decisions, and end up feeling lost. People are constantly telling us what they think and how we should live our lives, but you need to stop listening to them, trust yourself, and follow your dreams. Know who you are and what you are capable of and always trust one person—yourself—above everyone else.

Trust Yourself

IF YOU HAVE integrity and honesty, it will be easier for you to identify those traits in others you meet, making it easier to know who you can trust. Learn to trust yourself, live with integrity, and associate with people who share your values.

Decide what you want, and then decide not to stop until you get it. Even if the mistakes in life or the obstacles knock us down, we can always get back up. No one and nothing can hold you down unless you let it defeat you. Handing out my books in the United States, Canada, and all other English-speaking countries is one of my dreams. I recently gave a book to a client in Germany, and I was able to do this because I believed in myself enough to persist until I achieved my desired result. In Scandinavia, I have personally given out twenty-five books on nutrition, weight loss, and healthy living, and have sold more than 1.5 million books in Denmark, a country of only about 5 million people. That means that more that 25 percent of the population has purchased one of my books!

At the end of the day when your head hits the pillow, will you know that you spent your day moving closer to your dreams? This is not easy to do, but settling is much harder in the long run. Fall in love with a purpose for your life and get on track to fulfill that purpose. My purpose is to help as many people as possible do just that.

Confidence

YOUR HISTORY, YOUR environment, and your own value system shape the various aspects of your personality, and when you present yourself to the world as one person, that is not really in line with your true self, there are consequences. Portraying two selves can cost you dearly in terms of stress, energy, honesty, and confidence. There are as many definitions of and assumptions about confidence as there are people who write about it, research it, and long for it. Having healthy confidence means having a positive, affirmative, and constructive view of yourself. People with confidence believe in their capabilities, accept their strengths and limitations, set and work toward realistic goals, develop positive, rewarding relationships, and discover comfort in the world around themselves.

People who lack confidence tend to view themselves in a negative, pessimistic, and disapproving light, and are often unable to see beyond their limitations and problems. Low confidence levels are a mental health problem that can cause you to lose sight of your goals. It weakens your motivation, deprives you of meaningful relationships, and causes you to focus only on your limitations.

Unless you do something today to love yourself more, your position in life will be unchanged. Acquiring healthy confidence is more than saying, "I'm great." It is about setting goals and doing things to make yourself great. Confidence has less to do with feeling good than it has to do with feeling right. There is a substantial difference between the two. Feeling good won't always make you feel right, but feeling right will make you feel good every time. Good is a temporary emotion, but right is a solid knowing that no matter the outcome you performed in alignment with your beliefs as a person.

Confidence is as complex as the heavens, as vast as the desert, as deep as the oceans, and as fleeting as the wind. However, confidence is also as simple as setting a personal goal, working toward that goal with passion, focusing on the positive aspects of your life, and adhering to your personal sense of "right" as you travel your path.

Low confidence wanders into your life at the time and place of its choosing. It sometimes masks itself as depression, fear, or anxiety. This beast knows no boundaries and has a mind all its own. It is relentless until you learn how to recognize its approach, distinguish its footsteps on your porch, and deny its entrance into your life.

There is no "we" in confidence. Have you ever heard people talking about "our" confidence? In this voyage, you are on your own. I encourage you to seek the advice of loved ones, share your dreams and struggles, and talk about your advances and setbacks, but ultimately, there is only you. It is essential to your journey that you understand that no one but you can give you confidence.

The concept of confidence is abstract and intangible, but it is not an illusion. Healthy confidence is possible and real. Many people give up on confidence because they've never really tried to improve it, they've used incorrect techniques and advice, or they've allowed themselves to believe that it is a myth postulated by mystic healers. Confidence is real, and so is your journey.

People with healthy confidence find joy in recognizing others' worth as well. Confidence is about finding one's inner strengths and gifts, and using them to their fullest advantage. It is not about bragging and making yourself appear as more than you are—few things turn people off more than someone's unabated arrogance. Some people believe that if they can get a few people to love them (or even to merely like them), they will be validated as a person of worth. Confidence is about one type of validation only: self-validation. This means that you have come to terms with your worth and merit and that the only stamp of approval that you need is your own.

Think Positive

TO LIVE THE life of your dreams, you must be positive. You can't put off following your dreams because you're afraid something bad might happen. People with a positive attitude don't have the word tomorrow on their calendar. A positive attitude sets the tone for your day and, ultimately, for your life. I wake every morning around eight or nine o'clock and light candles around my bedroom to help wake me in a gentle and calming manner. As I sit in bed, I think about the day ahead of me, plan what I want to accomplish, and visualize it happening.

I always visualize a positive day ahead of me. If I had a bad experience the day before, I think about it, find the emotion that I connected to the event, and try to find out why I reacted the way I did. I think it is essential to take responsibility for your own personal growth and development; therefore, I make the best possible use of my quiet mornings, when there is time for reflection. A positive outlook on life attracts good to you. We all have desires and dreams, but without a positive mental attitude, we are only wishful thinkers. Positive thinking is the cement that bonds commitment and motivation, making your dreams come true.

Optimists believe that the positive events in their lives happen because of who they are, not what they do. Their optimism is internally based. They also have faith that the future will bring nothing but good things and that negative events are opportunities in disguise and should be used as learning experiences.

Pessimists, on the other hand, think that the bad events in their lives happen because of what they do. In contrast to the optimists, their pessimism is internally based as if the person is being picked on by life. They worry their future will be filled with one mishap after another and they view all positive events as serendipitous and unlikely to recur. Consider the people in your life—who among them do you prefer to spend your time with? The ones who constantly think the worst, or those who believe that anything is possible? A positive outlook on life is released through our personality and attracts people to us. Every day is a great day—don't just live for the weekends.

My job reflects my interests, so most of the time I don't feel like I'm working at all, which is one of the reasons I maintain such a positive outlook on life. I work at Lene Hansson's Wellness Center a few days a week, and I spend another few days writing books or working on my television program, *You Are What You Eat*. I am free every weekend and one spare day during the week, and I spend this time in our summer cottage by the sea, horseback riding and working with our dog, or simply having family and friends over and enjoying nature with my son.

My husband, Lars, runs the center on a daily basis, and there is a lot for him to do. We are now opening a smoothie bar as well, which connects to the center. He enjoys working there and has many great ideas for developing the health concept. I love to work with him and working side by side, we get to know each other better. We can now decide together how much we want to do, and when it's time for a holiday.

In the evening, I like to sit down to a healthy meal with my family, as my meals during the day consist mostly of fruits, vegetables, salads and other light health foods. Thrive on each moment you have, because once time passes, we can never get it back. I never want to look back on my life and say, "If only I had," or, "That should have been me." If you maintain a consistently positive attitude, I have no doubt you will look back on your life and say, "I lived my life to the fullest and have absolutely no regrets."

Pessimism is like a virus in your body. Once it takes command of your insides, a shutdown is inevitable. Worry, fear, doubt, and anxiety thrive in pessimistic environments. I can't imagine how many dreams have been lost to pessimism. Each of us has the world at our fingertips, and all we need to make them come true is a relentlessly positive attitude.

People often ask me how I can maintain such a positive attitude. It's simple; I tell them that I am an optimist because I believe that my life is unfolding exactly as it should be. I embrace the future, rather than fear it. Every person has a place in this universe. You may not know it, but someone in this world will be directly influenced by you. It could be someone as obvious as your children, or a total stranger, but we all make a difference in someone's life. As a positive person, you make life better for those around you. Before I read *Fit for Life,* I felt alone and helpless and as a result, was filled with negativity. It wasn't until I began to look deep inside myself, get healthy, and make a difference in this world that I realized how important a positive attitude is.

Lene Hansson

Every person's definition of success is different. For me, success was the moment back in 1991 when my publisher distributed my first book. I felt like all the hard work I'd done was being recognized. Since then, I've written twenty-five books on the subjects of nutrition, health, fitness, cooking, and many other related topics. My next big success came when Denmark's national television station asked me if I would take a job as the hostess of the show *You Are What You Eat.* Even though I had no experience, I took on the challenge because I believed in myself and had the confidence to go for it. Today, success is also in the small things, such as getting a massage or taking the time to meditate. Money isn't a measure of my success, all it means is that I can buy things.

Despite the various personal definitions of success, there is one universal quality that applies to each case: happiness. The truth is, you have to be unconditionally happy before you can find true success. Being happy just because your life is great and you have a successful business isn't enough—you must find happiness within yourself. Accept that you are not perfect, but recognize that behind the imperfections, you have a great deal of courage that will allow you to recover from any mistakes.

True happiness comes from within. It is not dependent on money, fame, or success. What makes me the happiest—and consequently, the most successful—is watching my son grow and have a happy, successful life of his own.

Babe in Purple

Lene Hansson
Babe in Purple

About Lene Hansson

LENE HANSON is a successful entrepreneur, speaker, author, and coach. She oversees the twelve employees of the Lene Hanson Wellness Center where they offer clients health consultations and work with them to help improve their nutrition. Along with her work at the Wellness Center, Lene produces a weekly television program You Are What You Eat and is currently working on a four part book that coincides with The Scandinavian Diet system to help people ward off unwanted weight and learn about the many diseases and illnesses associated with an imbalanced and unhealthy diet. In addition, Lene has developed a Scandinavian series of food products.

WEBSITE: www.lenehansson.com

BONUS GIFT:
"THE SCANDINAVIAN DIET" E book for only 5 € on the online store located on the website. Enjoy!

Babe in Purple

Babe in Orange

CHAPTER 12

Mona Jagga:
Babe in Orange

*"If it is to be, it is
up to me."*

— **Mona Jagga**

From the time I was a young child in India, I truly believed that
I was born to make a difference, and I was determined to get
through any circumstances and reach my goals. Immigrating to
Canada in 1993 was not easy. During my first few years here, I
worked as a cashier in an office supply store. I knew I was destined for more
and I stayed focused on finding my purpose. Even though I didn't yet know
what my purpose was, I envisioned myself empowering others to live the
lives of their dreams and desires.

I met and married my husband, a wonderful man named Arun, through an
arranged marriage. He was working in Saudi Arabia at the time, but he was
also originally from India, and as a couple we went through many financial
challenges as we started our life together. When I found out I was pregnant
in September of 1998, we were living in a tiny 500 square foot basement

apartment. I was determined to give birth to my child in my own house, so we purchased a 2,200 square foot house in January of 1999 and my son, Paras, was born five months later. Arun and I held several jobs and worked very hard to support our family, but deep down inside I knew I was born to do more.

Despite how busy this time was, I was always telling myself that I could work harder than everyone around me to achieve what I wanted. My ambition and drive were powered by my competitive spirit, and I finally quit my job, started my own business, and began to achieve success. No matter how successful I became, however, I was never completely satisfied within.

Deep down, I still felt that something was missing from my life, and this caused me to literally stop everything I was doing. Taking the time to reflect inwardly was incredibly empowering, and in doing so, I discovered the something that was missing.

I was living in a constant state of competition, which is not a natural or healthy state to be in. The part of me that had always wanted to help other people live their dreams and desires was rediscovered, and my purpose to empower women to tap into their natural feminine power was brought forth.

Find Your Purpose

I OFTEN REMIND my son that if Mahatma Gandhi had not tapped into his purpose, we may not have our independence today. If Mother Teresa had not tapped into her purpose, there may not be as much giving in the world today. If the Wright brothers had not tapped into their purpose, we might not have airplanes flying people from country to country. I never ask my son what he wants to be. I ask him, "What are you here for?" This opens up his way of thinking and encourages him to tap into his passion and purpose. So many people go about their daily lives doing what is required of them, but are still plagued by a nagging sense that there must be something more. If you feel like something is missing from your life, then you aren't living a life devoted to your purpose or passion. Your beliefs and values should center on what you are meant to do in this world, and deviating from these beliefs and values, or living according to someone else's wishes, leads you off your purposeful path.

Living a purposeful life involves total commitment. Obstacles are sure to arise in your path, but don't let them shake your confidence; instead, learn from them. Without challenges, you cannot fully appreciate your purpose, and your purpose is what will motivate you overcome all barriers and achieve what you love and live for. The satisfaction that comes from going through life knowing that you are living the life intended for you far outweighs the small obstacles you encounter on the way.

Don't let your culture, your current circumstances, your own inner dialogue, or anyone else's opinion of you limit your search for your purpose. Remember, this is your life, no one else's. Be patient, accept where you are on your life's journey, and when you succeed in consciously aligning your everyday life with your purpose, you will tap into unlimited reserves of wealth, empowerment, and success.

Train yourself to make your purpose the main focus of your life. If you have discovered the purpose that is right for you, devoting the necessary time should not be too difficult. It may take a bit of self-discipline at first, but your determination and faith will carry you through until it becomes a habit. By combining your purpose in life with an effort to work hard at achieving it, you are living your life to the fullest. We are all on this planet for a purpose, and we all have a gift to share with the universe.

Finding your purpose is like preparing your best dish to serve to others. Think about a buffet breakfast, lunch, or dinner. The best part about dining at a buffet is that you can choose from many dishes—this is ideal for a large group because the dish that will satisfy and fulfill you may not do the same for another person. Think of it this way: You have your own special dish to share with the world, made unique with your own special spices. If you don't bring your dish to the world, someone goes home starving. Only you have the recipe, so live your dream and passion—that is your purpose.

Purpose does not mean that one has to go out and empower others. Purpose simply means being fully satisfied within and knowing you are making a difference, whether that is in one person's life or the lives of many.

I n t u i t i o n

I WOULDN'T BE where I am today if I hadn't trusted myself and my intuition. I believe we all have the answers within us, and when I look back at the events of my life, I recognize that everything I attracted to myself had a purpose. I never define things as right or wrong, good or bad; instead, I consider them simply as events that help me move forward. If something doesn't go the way I expected, I simply ask myself why I attracted that situation and what lesson could I learn from it. I truly believe that we will continue to repeat lessons until we learn from them.

Not every investment I made was based on my intuition, and even though I have made some great profits, I also made some real estate investment decisions that did not turn out in my favor. These experiences were a catalyst for me to write my book, Stop…Don't Do It! The Ten Things You Must Know Before Risking Your Hard Earned Dollars in Real Estate. My goal in writing this book was to recount the hurdles I encountered so that other people wouldn't have to jump them. (www.stopdontdoitbook.com)

The universe teaches us through our intuition, and while I know this now, trusting my intuition hasn't always been at the forefront of my decision-making process. For many years, I was so busy looking for approval from others that I didn't listen to my own inner voice. My intuition would sometimes scream at me, but because I was so focused on expectations of other people, I didn't want to hear it. I really believe that all women are very intuitive—it is our natural feminine power. All I have to do is listen and make the decision; my intuition has an amazing ability to enable me to tap into my inner power. My intuition is an internal compass that tells me the best path to follow; I just need to trust it.

Quitting my job was not an easy decision to make. I was raising my five-year-old son, and we needed to pay his private school tuition, along with house costs, car payments, rent, and many other expenses. If it weren't for my trust in my feelings, I would never have had the faith to start my own business.

Whenever I need a solution for a troublesome situation, I close my eyes, ground myself, and step into the workshop in my mind. Inside, I'm able to free myself from the constraints of traditional thought processes and listen to my intuitive voice without any distractions. In my workshop, I often see important information that I tuned out during my busy day. Other times, I meditate to get in touch with my inner voice. Whatever method you choose, just realize that intuition is real and shouldn't be ignored. Our intuition is a profound gift that connects our embodied physical self with our higher power.

Giver's Gain

BEING AN ENTREPRENEUR is such a blessing for me; it provides the freedom, money, and success that allow me to make a difference in other people's lives. Creating new relationships is the most important force that contributes to my success and growth. I am always looking for ways to build meaningful relationships with people in order to help them achieve their dreams. If my support and encouragement can help someone achieve their goals, I believe my own blessings will increase. My business is about making a difference in the life of every person I come in contact with, whether through a personal connection, my book, an article, a phone call, or even through a ripple effect. I don't help others to make myself feel better—my true intention is to help other people realize that their own successes will make this world a better place and, in turn, I know I will also be rewarded.

Giving is a choice, and I only give what comes from a place of inner balance and harmony. This helps me be aware of any impulse-giving, which is not true giving. I believe that giving is the free-flow of universal activity, and the abundance out of which we overflow (in giving) is the abundance that is ours in the universe. The abundance I have will, out of necessity, flow out of me, and overflow to others.

To me the expression "the overflow of charity" is not just giving from the overflow of my assets, but the outgoing overflow of each of my actions; it isn't the amount of what I have given that gives me the inner feeling of satisfaction and cheerfulness. There is a privilege to being available to all that the universe wants me to do; it's available to all of us and it is a common privilege, not only to satisfy our "reason for being" through charity, but to be engaged together. We are all in it together! When one part of the universe is in need, we all have a need, until that part is supplied through others.

The universe provides a continuous supply that is available for giving. I want to make my dreams come true, but it's also very important to me that I give back to the world community in a big way. I have many dreams, and as I achieve them, I grow emotionally and financially, which allows me to continue to give. Everyday I talk to at least five or six of my many friends, and I have a stated goal of meeting five strangers each day.

I start everyday by telling myself that I am worthy, focused, and a powerful leader who is confidently creating balance and liberty in my life. I ask myself two questions before I do anything: Am I acting with integrity? Is this going to support others and make a difference in other people's lives?

I am a real estate professional, and before I show a house to a client, I ask myself, "Would I buy this property for myself?" If the answer is yes, I go for it, but if answer is no, I'm not going to waste my client's time. I apply the same principle to my seminars. I commit to others' success, because when I am committed to their success, they will be committed to mine. That is how the universe works. I can only attract what I give out, so if I want to be loved, I have to love myself first.

My life is about my choices. I refuse to blame circumstances, situations, or even people for negative situations—I take full responsibility. No matter what happens in my life, the meaning I give to the circumstances is up to me, and I do my best to make a story that urges me to move forward rather than one that pulls me back.

My husband and I have had much success as international real estate investors. Our success has given me the experience I needed to teach and inspire women to become aware of their own true inner power. My seminars and online webinars, Be a Wealthy Woman™, support and encourage women to empower themselves and find their purpose.

I want to share my knowledge with millions of people by traveling around the world and teaching women about their relationship with money. My desire is to help women create cash flow in their lives, so they can live an abundant life, take the necessary steps forward, and live the life of their dreams.

The challenges and difficulties I have faced have shaped the person I am today. My past experiences inspire me to value education for my own self-growth, and I am now truly living the life of my dreams and enjoying tremendous success.

My son is my greatest inspiration. I want to leave a legacy behind so that when I'm gone, my son can say that his mom lived a purposeful life. Despite being busy with seminars, webinars, and speaking events, plus working as a real estate professional, nothing keeps me from spending lots of quality time with my family.

I am always re-evaluating the techniques I use to educate others so that my services or products can be useful to as many people as possible. I want to educate them in a way that allows them to apply my lessons and experiences to their own lives and move forward. I am not concerned with people remembering who I am, I only want them to remember what I have taught them.

I believe that success is making all of your dreams come true, without compromising your happiness or losing your sense of self. My definition of success for my own life is related to being a woman, having a baby, becoming a mother, seeing my child raised with good values, being a loving daughter, being a loyal wife, and being a person who makes others smile in their darkest hour. I consider myself a success if I can live my life with integrity, morals, and values.

I live my life based on ten two-letter words: If it is to be, it is up to me. That affirmation makes me successful and responsible in my choices. It enables me to empower myself and those around me, and makes my life purposeful. Repeating those words to myself causes my dreams to become realities, and makes my goals and desires achievable.

Mona Jagga
Babe in Orange

About Mona Jagga

MONA JAGGA is a successful Real Estate Professional, author, and coach. For Mona, her true passion is to inspire women to follow their dreams. She specializes in seminars for Women in which she teaches them to release their self doubt, trust their intuition and become financially successful. Mona's new book, Stop! Don't Do It is a testament to her own success as well as a tool or anyone who wants to invest in Real Estate. Along with her Real Estate business, Mona volunteers for the nonprofit organization, PSI WORLD and devotes time to her community in a number of ways.

COMPANY NAME: Be A Wealthy Woman

WEBSITE: www.beawealthywoman.com

EMAIL: inspire@beawealthywoman.com

BONUS GIFT:
A ticket to a two day -live intensive seminar
valued at $497.00 & a one hour group coaching teleseminar.

Babe in Green

CHAPTER 13

Karen Lauderback:
Babe in Green

Surviving is important...
Thriving is Elegant

— Maya Angelou

When I was asked to contribute to this book, I thought it was a mistake. Who, me? I'm only on my way to success. People have always said that I'm lucky, or that the sun always shines on me, but I don't believe in luck, at least not in the traditional sense of the word. To me, LUCK stands for Laboring Under Correct Knowledge. I compare myself to some pretty amazing people and sometimes this makes me feel insignificant, but when I feel the need for inspiration or to be reminded of my greatness I go to the quote I have framed in my office by Marianne Williamson, said to be written for Nelson Mandela's 1994 inaugural speech: "Our deepest fear is not that we are inadequate. Our deepest fear is that we are powerful beyond measure. It is our light, not our darkness, that most frightens us. We ask ourselves, 'Who am I to be brilliant, gorgeous, talented, and fabulous?' Actually, who are you not to be? You are a child of God. Your playing small doesn't serve the world. There's nothing enlightened about shrinking so that other people won't feel insecure around you. We were born to make manifest the glory of God that is within us. It's not just in some of us; it's in every one of us. And as we let our light shine, we consciously give other people permission to do the same. As we are liberated from our fear, our presence automatically liberates others."

I soon remember that thinking about myself in negative terms doesn't serve anyone. So here I am, ready and willing to serve, with the hope that I can make a difference.

I've dreamed of becoming a nurse ever since I was in the fourth grade. My grandmother, aunt, and mother were all nurses, and I wanted to follow in their footsteps. I started college certain that I was going to be a nurse for the rest of my life, but soon the reality of my decision hit home. Not only did I not have the money to pay for my tuition, but there was an over abundance of nurses and my aunt was working overtime with no pay just to keep her job. The oversaturated field, and the thought of working evenings, weekends, and holidays and standing on my feet all day in a negative environment convinced me that nursing wasn't for me. Nevertheless, I still wanted to help people.

Shortly after this epiphany, a friend at a lending institution called me, and the next twenty-two years are history. My life had been given a purpose, as I was still doing something very real and helping people. I made more money in lending than I ever could have hoped to earn as a nurse. I was earning a six-figure income at the age of thirty, and most importantly, I loved what I was doing. I took the time to teach what I called "Mortgage 101" to my clients, so that they could make better choices. I helped some people with financial planning and helped others repair their credit and get on the path to homeownership. I obtained an insurance license and studied for series six and seven licenses, which are intended for stock brokering. I could see a bigger picture and I wanted to add more value to my client services. I believe that if you intend to be a professional, you have an obligation to know your industry. After all, that is why people come to a professional.

I don't attribute my success to doing certain things, but rather, to doing things in a certain way. In the mortgage industry, it was always my intention to treat everyone the way I would want to be treated. My boss once told me that I treated everyone as if they were the most important person at that moment. You can always find what you are looking for. I choose to look for the good, so that is what I found. After all, everything is just a reflection of what you are able to see.

I was named vice president of a large company and managed a partnership of approximately six hundred realtors, fifty investors, and twenty loan officers. I didn't get this position because I was the best educated or most experienced, but because I stepped in and did what needed to be done when the position became available. People at the top do not have a good attitude because they are at the top—they are at the top because they have a good attitude.

While I was with this company, my father got very sick. I was standing at the copier one day, and it occurred to me that he could be dying while I stood there. I packed some boxes of work to bring with me and left to go sit by his side. After two very special weeks with my family by his side, I gave him his last dose of morphine, and when they took his body away, I was left with my boxes. What a reality check. I knew something needed to change. I had two of my three miscarriages during that time and then, joyfully, had my third baby. I also considered filing for divorce. Experts advise us not to make major decisions during stressful times, and I knew I needed to get rid of some stress. My children represented unconditional love and true joy, and I wanted more of that love and joy in my life!

Freedom

THE FOLLOWING IS an entrepreneurial creed that filled me with inspiration when I first read it: "Like an eagle, I choose to soar to the highest heights for a view unknown by the vast majority of others. I do not choose to be a common person. It is my right to be uncommon. I seek opportunity, not security. I do not wish to be a kept citizen, humbled and dulled by having the state look after me. I want to take the calculated risk, to dream and to build, to fail, and to succeed. I refuse to barter incentive for a dole; I prefer the challenges of life to the guaranteed existence, and the thrill of fulfillment to the stale calm of Utopia. I will not trade my freedom for beneficence or my dignity for a handout. I will never cower before any master nor bend to any threat. It is my heritage to stand erect, proud, and unafraid—to think and act for myself, enjoy the benefit of my creations, and to face the world boldly and say: "This, with God's help, I have done". "All this is what it means to be an entrepreneur." (Author unknown)

Hundreds of years ago, everyone was self-employed. Eventually, people began specializing and trading, which evolved into going to school, getting a job, and "giving your boss a good day's work for your wages." At sixty-five or so, you'd retire and collect a pension, retirement, or social security. Those days are over. Young people today will not only change jobs many times, they will change careers several times as well! The world is ever changing and I believe "the only one sure thing is change." This is evolution. People can be trained, retrained, or educated very easily. As one generation is elevated, it leaves room for the next generation to grow.

Back when most people were self-employed, their networks consisted of their family, friends, church members, and townspeople. Today, an entrepreneur's network is the entire world, which seems to be getting smaller every day. You can teach someone across the world to complete a task for a fraction of what it costs in North America. This has led to both out sourcing and in sourcing. Rather than losing jobs, it has opened the possibility for more creativity with jobs. As an entrepreneur, you should never spend time doing anything that you can hire someone else to do. Our country continues to evolve in services and consulting to other countries as they go through their industrial revolution. As a global economy, other countries are able to complete smaller tasks elevating our laborers to participate in creating the "bigger pie."

For example, in our GAC (Global Aggregation Corporation), our ultimate goal is to raise entrepreneurs so high that ten million people are elevated to another level to fill the space they leave behind. Create a bigger pie and everyone can have a bigger piece!

I decided to become an entrepreneur for many reasons. I wanted to work from home, make unlimited money, and help others do the same. Most of all, I wanted freedom! I know a lot of successful people, but not many of them can teach others to do the same and to enjoy the lifestyle I have. Originally, I wanted a balanced life, but I now believe that balance is not the goal. Harmony feels like a better word. If I had the chance to start my career over again, I would become an entrepreneur much sooner! The view is so different with the lights on. People living in survival mode are crawling on the floor with only a flashlight, trying to see what is directly in front of them. An entrepreneur walks in and turns on the floodlights, exposing a whole new world. A new vision!

An entrepreneur is like a soaring eagle. Both are leaders who are brave enough to fly alone and influence others. With great knowledge comes great power, and with great power comes great responsibility. Our God-given talents were given to us to be used. It may be easier to follow the crowd. You may be using your talent along with the masses or in a crowd like a musician. If it feels natural and you are good at it then continue. But if you want to try your hand at owning a business and owning your life, there are ways to start without leaving your JOB (Just Over Broke). You can get started with very little funds and very little risk depending on the opportunity you choose. You may consider relationship marketing. I call it the SHIPping and receiving business. You build relationSHIPs that lead to friendSHIPs that lead to partnerSHIPs that lead to leaderSHIPs. You can choose to distribute any product anywhere in the world, build the network distribution structure for it and enjoy RECEIVING repeat residual income and freedom! What I love most about being an entrepreneur is the freedom! I enjoy every moment and I am 100 percent responsible for myself. Who would want someone else to be responsible for them? To them, yes, but not for them. You may learn more at our web site www.networktocracy.com.

I believe certain magnates used their influence to cut entrepreneurial philosophy from the curriculum of the educational system. This kept folks seeking employment, and ensured that they would be willing to "give their boss a good day's work for their wages." In my mind, trading time for money is the worst possible strategy for creating wealth, yet 96 percent of the population uses this strategy. They go to work, trading time for money but earn only 1 percent of the money. A further 3 percent of the population uses their assets to create more income, earning three percent of the world's wealth, and 1 percent of the population earns 96 percent of the world's money by using the multiple source of income strategy. Bob Proctor was the first to expose me to this awareness and strategy.

If you were to ask a group of third graders, "Who would like a job?" how do you think they would answer? Let me tell you what a job is. A job tells you when to get up in the morning, when to go to work, when to eat lunch, and when to take a break. It tells you when to go home and whom to work with, whether or not you like them. A job tells you when you will take vacation, how long your vacation will be, how much you will be paid, and how much you are worth. After you have traded time for money for years, you may not have anything to show for it. A retirement plan may or may not be there for you, even if it was promised.

Now, who wants a job? No self-respecting third grader would raise their hand. Their minds are still active and creative, and they believe that they can do anything. In fact, they can. When does this thinking change? When is the desire to do what you want to do become extinguished? When does the desire to follow your heart's passion and use your God-given talents get buried?

No man is kept from progressing, or held back except by the limitations in his own mind. You may feel like your options are limited, but no one can hurt you or keep you down unless you let them. No one can take away your free will. Your thoughts become your words, your words become your actions, your actions become your results, your results become your character and your character becomes your destiny. You decide what you want to do with your life, and God's answer will always be, "Yes, yes, YES!"

Becoming an entrepreneur is not the easiest, most popular, or safest path, but it is— in my opinion—the best path. Before you take the first step, ask yourself what you really want. If times get challenging, you will need to remember YOUR why (WHY YOU

WANT IT) to keep yourself on track. So, what do you really, really want? When you ask questions, the universe always answers. I call this afformation, not affirmation, because you are forming something new. When you repeat affirmations, your subconscious mind can sometimes contradict you. ("You can't do that!") This is a case of the ant controlling the elephant. An afformation, on the other hand, asks, "How?" Take any negative thought that is playing in your head, turn it into a question, and see what happens!

In "The Great Little Book of Afformations" Noah St. John & Denise Berard explain that an affirmation is a statement of something you would like to be true in your life. The problem is many of us doubt our own affirmations because we try to convince ourselves of something we don't believe is true. They state in this little book, and I agree, that the human mind operates by asking and answering questions. You ask a question and your mind searches for the answer.

They suggest you take the 5 most disempowering questions you hear in your head and start asking 5 new empowering questions.

For example:

1) Why can't I do any thing right?/How is it so easy and so okay for me to have, do and be anything I want?

2) Why can't I get any new referrals?/How do I get referrals every day?

3) Why do these things always happen to me?/How am I such a success?

4) Why am I so lonely?/How am I so loved?

5) Why are my kids always fighting?/How can my kids be so loving and helpful? I simply started with "How can it get any better than this" and the communication inside and outside of myself was in harmony and the answers came and keep coming!

Take the time to define your passion and focus on what you do well. Set your goals. Plan the work, then work the plan. Keep moving in the direction of your dreams, and don't look right or left. Don't talk to your neighbor about what you should do. Too many people wonder what their neighbors will think. Don't worry, they don't think. Most people would rather die than think and as a matter of fact they do. Thinking is some of the hardest work you will ever do. Thinking is one of the few things that separates us from animals. God's gift to you is more talent and ability than you could ever use in a lifetime. Your gift to God in return is to use that talent and ability to its fullest extent. You know your truth. As Shakespeare said, "Above all, to thine own self be true!"

If you want to have a good partner, "be" a good partner. If you want to have good business, then "do" good business. If you want to have a good friend, "be" a good friend. "Be" first. Then "do" and you will have. Model what you want, transfer your vision to others, and build people, a team of people. It takes years to build a person. Think of a college degree or a masters or management program or raising a child. One plus one can be much more than two, when you add synergy. The more I learn, the more I realize how much I don't know, so it's important to be open-minded. Co-create.

Discover your life's purpose and live it! I love what I do, so it doesn't feel like I'm working—every day feels like a Saturday. I am following my purpose of creating healthy environments for people all over the planet. I may be doing many things, but combined, they create my one ultimate goal of fulfilling my purpose.

Life's Lessons

EVEN IN THE midst of challenges, I truly appreciate the lessons I'm able to learn from them. When the lessons are particularly difficult, I thank God. I tell myself, "God must think I'm really great if I'm good enough to handle this one."

I started in business as a babysitter when I was ten years old. The parents of the first little girl I looked after assumed I was much older and were surprised to learn my actual age. I always looked for ways to be helpful. I cut the grass, shoveled snow, and assisted with a paper route. I volunteered for many events through Camp Fire Girls, 4H, church, and school events. It is in giving that we receive, and the amount of service determines the reward.

During the mid-80s, I worked for a local savings and loan. I had a very real, very difficult experience at this job. As people became nervous about the security of their money, there was a run on the local savings and loan. We had to lock the doors and tell people that they could not have their money. A lesson in the bigger picture is that the only real security comes through cash flow, not through hording money and hoping it will be there or thinking the government is going to take care of everything. I remember the panic and the fear in the eyes of the customers and the employees as the institutions they believed in were revealed as insolvent. People stood scared at the doors believing their life savings were inside. We did not know how far they would take their anger or if they were armed. I believe we receive the same lesson repeatedly until we learn it, so when I am given new challenges, I look at it as a gift because I must be rising to a higher level of consciousness to be receiving greater challenges. And believe me, I've had my share and then some!

I have also had many honors in business. I've always loved what I chose to do, and I'm always excited about what might come next. When Frank Lloyd Wright was asked what his favorite project was, he answered, "The next one." When you enjoy each moment, the moments become hours, and the hours become days, always getting better and better! If each moment is good, then each day is good. I have been very blessed to do what I love and travel the world with my love, my children, and wonderful like-minded and interesting people.

I have had many moments of awe and appreciation in my professional life. I suppose I expect the best, and it comes to me. I have been blessed to learn directly from, and spend time with, incredible teachers such as Bob and Linda Proctor, James Ray, Michael Beckwith, Mark Victor Hansen, Jack Canfield, Jay Abraham, Gordon Bizar, Doug Wead, Stephen Shapiro, Robert

Kiyasaki, Hilton Johnson, Phia Kushi, Sir Alan Mooney and my fiancé Dr. Roger Boger. I'm also thankful for the opportunities I've had to learn indirectly from many others who are all on a high level of vibration. I listen to many teachers, but when I have the chance to have a direct conversation; attend a private meeting, worship service, or cruise; or share a drink, dinner, dance, or even a thought, I consider myself very honored. I only hope that I can learn enough to share with others, so that I can leave them with the same impression of increase that the amazing folks listed above left on me.

The Bigger Picture

WITH UNSHAKEABLE BELIEFS, you can do anything. When you make a committed decision, the universe will move in your direction. When you have faith in yourself, your product or service, and your company or industry, you will attract everything you need. If you do not have this belief or vibration yet then look for someone to work with or choose a mentor who does. Others will feel their vibration until they feel it from you. When you are communicating from this level of vibration, it doesn't matter what you say. Spoken words make up only 7% of communication—everything else is communicated through the vibration of who we are. I choose the vibration of love. Love is not a verb, something you do. It is a noun, who you are. People won't remember everything you say, but they will remember how you made them feel. People you work with are affected by you and you by them.

I am fortunate enough to be able to choose the people I work with. Be careful in your choices of who you spend time with. People come in and out of our lives for a reason, a season or a lifetime. If someone brings you down, then you are not your best, and how can you serve the world when you're not at your best? Acknowledge the lesson learned and move on. I work with clients globally. I choose where and when I spend my time. I try to use technology for effective communication as much as possible. When I am not traveling I work from home, where I am constantly inspired by being near my children and the love of my life, Roger, who keeps me in a state of gratitude. Whenever possible Roger and I travel together and take the children when we can.

Surround yourself with people who inspire and motivate you. Look to work with people you like and who like you. Look for people who want what you have and they will be so happy they met you. They will feel so good when they buy what you have because they have been looking for it.

If you want to radiate a buying vibration, think of the last time you bought something that you were really excited about. Maybe it was a gift for someone and you felt great about it. Remember the smell of that new car or the feel of those great new shoes. Now you are in the buying vibration. When you want to sell something, don't think about how to sell it, but about how great someone will feel when they own it.

Use pull marketing, not push marketing. Create the things that people want and they will pull you to them because you can give them those things. Don't push what you have on people just because you have it to sell, look for people who want what you have.

When you're talking to a customer, treat the conversation like an interview where the goal is to find out what they are looking for. You know what you can offer them, and you don't want to waste your time or theirs, trying to sell them a product or service they don't want. You are looking to see if what you offer and what they want is a match, so you can close the sale or move on. If you are nervous, you are thinking only of yourself and what they think of you. If you are truly concerned with their best interests, you won't be nervous because it is not about you. If you get nervous, this is emotional guidance telling you that you're approaching the situation with the wrong intention.

It is important to acknowledge that we all have the same amount of time. We can't save or manage time but we can manage activity. Make a list and prioritize. Consider the attitude of what you "want to" do or get done today, not what you "have to" do. Feel the difference? Avoid energy vampires who can drain your positive feelings with their negative talk and emotions, and for God's sake, don't be one!

I am so much more effective when I enjoy the activity I am doing. Find your purpose, what you love to do, and do that! If circumstances keep you from doing it now, set a plan and work toward that moment in time. Operate with the knowledge that everything you do is now working in the direction of your dream. You are either moving forward or backward, growing or dying. If it feels good, move toward it, and if it feels bad, move away from it. This is your emotional guidance system—use it! When you continue moving forward, you will soon find yourself stepping into that place in time and that time is now!

Consider that if you save too much money, you may stop the flow. Money is just green energy, flowing to us and through us. It is not the money we want, it is the things that the money can get us. Have a plan and have confidence in God's Law of Abundance. Be willing to take risks. Does it feel right? Is your action in the direction of your dreams? What are you afraid of? What is holding you back? Will it harm someone else? Is it ethical? If you fail at the first attempt, will you be out on the street? You may know of people on the street but do you believe you will be one of them if you take this action? Will you be without food? Will you lose a valuable relationship? If you answered no to the above questions, then make a decision to take action in that direction. The only mistake you can make is to do nothing. Success is the progressive realization of a worthy ideal!

Have multiple sources of income (MSIs). The most money you will ever lose is the money you did not make. The more risk you take the higher the payout can be, but of course, with greater risk comes the greater chance of losing what you may already have . Participating in the global economy and diversifying your investments are options that can help you balance out the risk factor. If you don't know how to play the game don't play it. Learn tax avoidance, not tax evasion. There are many benefits to being an entrepreneur. Profits are better than wages. Be knowledgeable and surround yourself with knowledgeable people. Take classes, read books, have intelligent conversations, and listen!

Save at least 10% of your income, and give another percent away. You decide the percent and to whom you give it to. It is in giving that we receive. Choose who you believe will benefit the most and who you feel good about helping. This will also help you to make the appropriate decisions when so many organizations ask for you to give them your hard earned money. Keep it flowing! People of the Jewish faith teach their children about money and abundance at a very young age. For example, if they give a child a gift of $10, they'll give ten one-dollar bills, not one ten-dollar bill. With ten one dollar bills, they can easily save ten percent, give ten percent, and keep or use the rest. This is a great example that follows what many believe is God's law or faith regarding the use of money, which states that we should tithe 10% of our abundance. The important thing is to follow your belief because you create your world. I believe we are rewarded in direct proportion to our services.

With this lesson in mind, use the percentage intended for you, but don't purchase something unless you love it. For example, don't settle for clothes that don't feel good. Even if you get them at a great price, if you don't wear the items, you've wasted your money. Mix a few really nice items with some general items—just enough to feel the quality. Not every piece needs to be top dollar, but appreciate everything and you will feel better about it. Remember, it is the feeling that is paramount. As Tony Robbins would say, "Everything that people do is to avoid pain or gain pleasure."

There are times when you are so close to something, your vision is blurred. If you step back and look at the bigger picture, everything becomes much clearer. More importantly, you can see where you fit in the picture. We are the center of our universe, and taking care of ourselves is a good thing. My goal is to be inter-dependant, not dependant, independent or co-dependant. Being selfish is not just living the way you want to live; it is forcing others to live the way you want to live as well. God wants you to live in abundance.

All human behavior is learned, so question your paradigms. I follow what I believe to be the 7 natural laws of the universe: perpetual transmutation, relativity, vibration and its sub law attraction, polarity, rhythm, cause and effect, and gender. One of my favorites is the Law of Attraction, which states that your thoughts become things. Another favorite of mine is the Law of Relativity, which basically states that nothing is except your thinking makes it so. I believe that if you do not earn your riches in accordance with God's law, they will not bring you happiness and they will be fleeting.

What actually happens to you in life is not as important as how you handle it. I have learned that tears are emotional guidance. I listen to my inner voice and I've made it this far by making decisions, setting goals, taking action, and having belief and gratitude. The idea of "getting to the top" is relative. You can only see so far, and when you reach what you thought was the top, there will be another mountain that you could not see before.

Eleanor Roosevelt said, "Great minds discuss ideas, average minds discuss events, and small minds discuss people." I love spending time creating solutions with people. Albert Einstein said, "If I give you a penny, you will be one penny richer and I will be one penny poorer. If I give you an idea, you will have a new idea, but I shall still have it too." I believe that there is an abundance of money in the world, but a shortage of people who teach others how to attract it. Attracting ideas is a little harder, but people are the greatest asset.

My last name, Lauderback, means clear water. It is an acquired name that I share with my children so I have kept it to this point. Ironically, my big-picture goal is to be part of a team that directs or controls funds to aid in the future water crisis and other global issues. I believe the human race's evolution is threatened due to our diets. We are what we eat, digest, assimilate and excrete. This is creating unhealthy condition in too many people. It is not who they are but their condition causing all of the disorders. This can be corrected. I believe I will continue on this path for the rest of my life which I fully expect to be over 100! As Sandra Bullock said in Miss Congeniality, "I really do want to save the world." Most people want the same three things: They want to be loved, they want to be part of something bigger than they are and they want to make a difference.

If you would like to know more, you can find me at www.Networktocracy.com. This is the platform where I will continue to find and grow an empire of empire builders who want to be part of something bigger than they are. Here, you will find solutions partners who will assist you on your journey. I intend to use some of their vehicles to share what I have learned with others. I feel responsible for bringing awareness to people; it is then their job to choose. I am not attached to a particular outcome for any person's choices. The good news is that we don't all want the same things. I only want to help people achieve the outcomes that they desire.

I am a combination of my experiences and in life's journey. I believe it is the lessons that are the most valuable. In familiar people, we find ourselves. In the end it is the relationships that matter most. I love the anonymous quote, "To the world you may be one person, but to one person you may be the world." What a worthy ideal! My relationships with my family, friends, clients, society, and especially with the greatest children a mother could wish for Brad, Mitch, Leah, Aiden, and my future husband Roger, have made me what I am today. Everyday I am reminded that in the middle of an ordinary life, there are miracles. And every day I enjoy more of the reality of the life I have always dreamed of. I continually pray for a healthy body, mind, soul, family, society, and finances. I celebrate life, expect goodness, choose happiness, and stay in gratitude. My intention is to model this to the world, and with this vision my wish is that others will do the same. Imagine that!

Karen Lauderback
Babe in Green

About Karen Lauderback

KAREN LAUDERBACK has extensive training in management, sales, marketing and self development. As the owner of Magnificent Balance, she empowers individuals to achieve health, wellness, and balance in their life. With her past experience in the banking industry, Karen is also able to help others acquire personal and financial success as a Life Coach. She and her husband have over twenty Multiple Sources of Income, and has recently begun work on her Series Seven License to help foster the growth of their latest MLM Company, Diamond Tree. Karen is also a core team leader of the GAC Global Aggregation Corporation.

FULL NAME: Karen E Lauderback

COMPANY NAME: Networktocracy

WEBSITE: www.KarenLauderback.com

EMAIL: Karen@KarenLauderback.com

BONUS GIFT:
Free 20 minutes of coaching.

Babe in Blu

CHAPTER 14

Sydney Blu:
Babe in Blu

Always work hard and never stop.
When you stop, life stops.

A ll of my life, I never had a doubt about becoming a Dj. Something inside told me that I would be great. Since I was a young girl, I always loved to perform. Inspired during my college years in Ottawa, Ontario, I started performing live in 2000. The Atomic Nightclub was known for having the best Dj's in the world on Saturday night. The more I watched them, the more I wanted to be onstage. I aspired to be the best in the business. For me this wasn't just a hobby, this was going to be my life. It was all or nothing.

After graduating, I moved to Toronto and spent some time waitressing. As a matter of fact, I stashed my waitressing tips in a wine bottle so that I could buy my first set of turntables. After noticing an ad for a financing company in the back of a magazine, I realized this could be a good way of getting my decks quickly, so I submitted a credit application and bought my first set of decks. During my stint as a waitress, I contemplated taking a job in the travel industry until I got my first gig. I did so well and got another one immediately. This was the beginning of my career as a professional Dj.

Now, I play for thousands of people who love my music. For them, both my shows and music are memorable experiences. I've had incredible shows in Spain when I played Space Ibiza, the number one nightclub in the world. I also have had some amazing shows in Miami, New York City, Mexico and in my hometown of Toronto. My song Give It Up for Me (one of my biggest hits to date) went to number one on the Electro house chart on Beatport (the #1 dance music retailer in the world) and was in the top 10 for 2 months. At the end of 2008 it was named the number eight song of the entire year.

M o v e   F o r w a r d

AS I WAS making a name for myself in this industry, I wanted to avoid one of the most common mistakes people make. Far too often a person can waste tremendous amounts of time on activities that don't move them forward. This is true for any career, not just music. I learned as I went along what was taking me forward and what was keeping me still. Two phenomenal books helped me along the way. The first one, *Last Night a DJ Saved My Life* is a story about the history of the disk jockey. This book helped me to learn the roots of the Dj business. My favorite and most inspiring book, *The Paradise Garage* was a valuable tool in learning the origins of house music.

A lot of people try different angles on "making it" in my industry but the bottom line is you must produce great music, market yourself well and put on a good show. I had to learn all of these lessons in order to get signed with my agency and move forward. I am constantly researching my industry, reading about new technologies and making every attempt to learn how I can improve. This is essential. For me, each lesson came one at a time but now all of these factors are what make me successful. Just as I read books related to my chosen field, you also need to research whatever business you're considering.

Choosing an interesting and rewarding career involves identifying your skills, interests and values, plus lots of career exploration. Self-assessment can help define your needs and abilities, what kind of work you want to do and the type of setting you would be happy in. A great way to find out information is to talk to those who are already working in the field you're interested in. Knowing what's happening in your target job market makes it much easier to make an informed decision and makes you aware of all the possibilities available to you. By taking the time to do your research, you will have many more options in both your personal fulfillment and your level of income. Once you find someone whose job interests you, spend time with them and ask them to show you the in's and out's of their business.

A Strong Work Ethic

I LIVE BY the code of ethics to always work hard, and be kind to others. If you don't treat people with respect your talents and skills mean nothing. If I'm passionate about something, I'm good at it. That's the bottom line with me. It's an inner drive that comes out of you and makes you work for what you want for yourself and your life. I met my initial goals due to a strong work ethic. I do however; think I still have ways to go. I want to travel to more parts of the world and become better known in other markets such as Asia, Australia and other parts of Europe. I want to sell more records and in turn make my record label become one of the biggest labels in the world. My work ethic pushes me to continue to build my 'BLU' empire and very soon, the words Sydney Blu will be internationally known.

If you want to make more of yourself and our life, it is essential to develop a strong work ethic. A person, who works hard and is eager and willing, will almost certainly be noticed by the people who can help. I don't stop to smell the roses. I am always looking for what's next to learn, what's next to take me forward. I don't get comfortable because that is when things start to slow down, and I have so much more to accomplish!

Prepare yourself to ignore the negative attitudes of peers and colleagues who prefer to take the easy option of doing the minimum amount required to get by. This is really only an option if you have no interest in self-improvement or building a better life for yourself. I love the satisfaction of writing music and watching the expressions on my audience's faces. The most rewarding aspect of my hard work is knowing that my music resonates with the audience.

Madonna is definitely my inspiration because she has had a long road of success and learned so much on the way. I believe this to be an example of myself (having so much more to still accomplish). My career will encompass my life and I am always open to learning, improving and reinventing myself.

There are plenty of people who pride themselves on doing as little as possible, beating the system or getting one over on management. Politics are all over the music industry. Tons of artists create drama for themselves because of jealousy and because their success is not as good as someone else's. Those who are even worse are the ones who are jealous because of the success of a woman. Sometimes I've felt ganged up on because people were angry I was getting more gigs than them. I've also felt resented because of the fact that I work hard to reap the benefits instead of sitting back and watching life go by. I've always had a strong work ethic and this is the reason for my success

Emotional Armor

IN THE PAST, I had some difficulty dealing with people. When I was younger I was fairly emotional, which made it hard to handle certain business situations. Young and vulnerable, I soon realized that I needed to toughen up and develop a thick skin. Criticism can come from peers, mentors, editors, parents, the media, and anyone else who might be privy to your work. It can be devastating and potentially prevent you from achieving your dreams.

It is difficult to succeed if you let every little word "get" to you. It is crucial to develop some armor. Developing a sense of what's being said to you, why, and what response you should make, may take some doing but it will make you more skillful when dealing with people in your working environment. Having a thick skin, however, doesn't mean cultivating the tendency to just tune everything and everyone out. Instead it teaches you how to be the most professional you can be in a difficult situation.

One important piece of advice I'd like to offer is that it's not all about you. By this I mean, when someone makes a hurtful comment, they are more likely experiencing their own personal issues bringing them down. Unfortunately, you are just an outlet for their frustrations. Always remember that everyone is watching, not just those above you. And they notice more than your day-to-day performance. Strength, self-confidence, and an unwillingness to be petty will not go unnoticed and will bring you respect.

Professionalism should always be attached to your thick skin. How you present yourself before, during and after business hours is your true character. Diplomacy plays a big part. At times there may be a few personalities that collide and it's during those moments where you have to put on your protective armor and also be a diplomat. We need to distinguish ourselves from our critics by maintaining some degree of composure.

I have made many mistakes throughout the course of my career, yet I have always maintained my dignity and a certain level of professionalism. One mistake that comes to mind is when I combined a personal relationship with business. I once dated my manager and then dated a guy who I wrote music with and joined his record label. Although this might seem like it had its perks at the time or even a natural progression because you share the same passion, it was really a bad idea. Personal and business relationships should always be separate. I could teach a seminar on this now! Never threaten what you've worked hard for by compromising it for a personal relationship. Most importantly, never let someone you are involved with personally handle your career. It's just a recipe for disaster. You own that. No one else. Independence is the most attractive aspect about being a strong woman.

Thick skin, criticism, professionalism, and mistakes. All of these are just part of being in business. But working for myself, doing what I love, and performing for people who I inspire, make the bad disappear and magnify all that's right with life. There's nothing like having someone tell you that you made their night or send you an email about how much you have inspired them. It's an unbelievable feeling. The ability to perform for thousands of people. The satisfaction of this is priceless. It's what I've always done well and I wouldn't do anything different. Life unfolds perfectly and I've learned a good deal. Yes, I didn't do everything perfectly but I think there's a reason for mistakes... you learn from them. I hope my story has inspired you and remember, the key to ultimate happiness is fulfilling your dreams.

Joanne Hill

aka Sydney Blu

Babe in Blu

Sydney Blu Biography

One of the finest female artists of her generation, Sydney Blu's transformation from bedroom obscurity to global recognition has been nothing short of spectacular. She sits high on the list of global labels with her sound onto the latest releases and a Dj'ing schedule in over 36 countries across 5 continents. In 2004, her first compilation YTO 2004 became one of Canada's top releases of the year and was instantly catapulted into the minds of the electronic music world. In the following years, Sidney cemented her position as one of the top female producers with labels such as Hi Bias, Double Frequency Records, PBR Recordings, Don't Look Productions, and Rawthentic Music and various others. In early 2008, Sydney completed her biggest track to date in Give It Up For which rocketed to the number one spot on Beatport's Electro chart and 3 on Beatport's main chart. She is the only female artist to ever have a top ten hit on the Beatport charts and is expected to have many more this upcoming year coming on her own label Blu Music.

FULL NAME: JOANNE HILL aka SYDNEY BLU

COMPANY NAME: BLU MUSIC

WEBSITE:
www.sydneyblu.com, www.myspace.com/djsydneyblu

EMAIL: sydney@sydneyblu.com

BONUS GIFT:
Free Mixed CD

Babe in Chocolate

CHAPTER 15

Felicia Pizzonia:
Babe in Chocolate

"Desire is the starting point of all achievement, not a hope, not a wish, but a keen pulsating desire which transcends everything."
— **Napoleon Hill**

The bottom of a pyramid is always crowded and a hard place to find good breathing room. I realized this early in my teenage years and decided that there is plenty of room at the top, and that that is where I want to be. Life is a beautiful adventure and the only way to have fun is to do what you love. The rest will follow. As it is written in the Scriptures, you will reap what you sow. Living your life with purpose and passion, plants the seeds for integrity, blessings, and fulfillment.

After finishing high school, I took a year off to earn some money to pay for college. During that time, I worked for a telemarketing firm and had to make three hundred calls a day on an automatic dialer. I actually thought this was fun, and I would play around with accents and different voices. I turned out to be really good at it! Soon the fun started to fade, but by that time, I had realized that I was a persuasive salesperson with unexpectedly good communication skills. For someone barely out of high school interested in health and business, finding that I had a unique sales ability, a lucrative talent was an amazing revelation for a teen!

I decided to take my newly discovered talents and go to work for an advertising agency. The world of advertising was the perfect environment for me. I was able to combine my love of creativity with my sales and communication skills, and I flourished like an orchid in a hot house. I knew, however, that despite how well situated as I was, I was destined to do more with my life than just work for someone else and dance to the tune they were playing. I wanted my own stage, my own orchestra, and I even wanted to write my own music.

I learned about the budgeting process for brands, and honed my ability to create a unique and impactful advertising vehicle that offered a high return on the client's investment. Once I'd refined these skills, I started my own agency. Needless to say, if there was anything I was lacking, it was neither pride nor ambition. I was convinced that my agency would succeed, and lo and behold, it did.

By the time I was twenty-three, I had accomplished more than most people twice my age. I owned my own successful advertising agency specializing in trade shows and niche markets. I was always willing, anxious even, to improve my business and myself so I learned an incredible amount of information on developing innovative strategies that offer businesses a high return on their advertising and marketing dollars. I invested in Tony Robbins' Sales Mastery Course and read his book, *Awaken the Giant Within.* I was also blessed by meeting one of my mentors, Tasso Lakas, a brilliant media mind who encouraged me to be confident and never to doubt myself. He was tough on me and told me to read more books and expand my vocabulary; however, he also complimented me when he saw merit and admitted that he had nothing to teach me about sales presentations or telesales, he thought I was a sales superstar. Throughout my life, I've always had a passion for business and entrepreneurial projects. The only thing that was missing was the fact that I did not realize that the journey was the destination so I was not having fun and burned out quickly in 2004 since I was too focused on the goal. So, now rather than having goals, I have a promise plan, a small card that I write my detailed goals on or promises to myself with a date to achieve it. I recite my promise card and feel the feelings as though my goals have already occurred in the present. It is important to pick your passion and follow your heart.

PROMISE PLAN CARD

I am so happy and grateful now that I have set up four meetings daily with entrepreneurs or CEO`s who understand the value of marketing and would like to publish a book with the Ultimate Publishing House.

I am so happy and grateful now that I have my house on the water and have placed a deposit by March 5th, 2010.

You can create your own promise plan card and carry it with you, so you can refer to it daily.

What I love about being an entrepreneur, —and still do—is having an idea, then creating and implementing it and reaping the benefits of the completed work. I realized early on that it is not the things you do, but the way you do them. All the difference lies in whether you go above and beyond the line of duty with passion, enthusiasm, and the sincere effort to add value to others and their businesses. An interesting sidebar is that by profession, I am a registered nutritionist; however, I have always had a God-given talent: the ability to communicate with passion and persuasion. I believe that my talent lies in the way I unfailingly speak the truth, straight from the heart. I speak with people and remember their essence, who we are by going back to being three years old since that is our true being. Unlike many people in business, I have no patience or respect for artifice or other legerdemain common to the industry. I went on to work with some amazing publishing houses and trade show companies, as well as media houses in Toronto, Canada. I also had the pleasure and honor of working with such industry giants as Tony Robbins, Bob Proctor, and Les Brown.

I've always dreamed of working with the amazing Louise Hay, founder of Hay House and pioneer of the self-help movement. I aspire to be the next Hay House with my company, the Ultimate Publishing House, a book publishing company that has fused publishing, branding and publicity all in one. At eighty years old, Louise Hay is a dynamic and legendary figure, but one who certainly had her share of trials and tribulations. Most people in her shoes would have given up; instead, she developed her own highly successful publishing house, one of the top in the world, leading in self-help, mind, body and spirit books.

The Ultimate Publishing House also known as TUPH specializes in book publishing that offers instant credibility, visibility and distinction so the author uses the book as a marketing tool. TUPH also help authors establish multiple streams of passive income through a marvelous system that includes: author blogs, publicity, press release and radio and talk show bookings and plenty more. Getting the book is the easy part, the process is less than six months and the end product is stunning, since the TUPH team stands behind you the entire journey to being a published author. I am very passionate about the publishing industry, and it is near and dear to my heart. Being a published author is a prestigious title and worthy of celebration, but most of all, it is lots of fun.

The establishment of my own publishing house, with offices in Toronto, Canada, Houston, Texas as well as Columbus, Ohio, was a natural flow of my passion for all things written, coupled with my extensive background in media and advertising. The two worlds collided and The Ultimate Publishing House (also known as TUPH) was born.

TUPH's mission is to help people promote their business or specialty field by enabling them to publish a book that they can use as their ultimate branding and marketing tool. In by publishing a book, the author is able to establish instant credibility, gain public and media visibility, enjoy the distinction of being a published author, while the publication positions them as experts in their chosen field. Their book will help them market their ideas or business, attract more clients, and drastically increase their income!

It is particularly rewarding for me to know that my unique and cutting-edge marketing process is helping authors increase their business and make a better life for themselves and their family. I don't just publish books; I help fulfill dreams. When you add value with pure intent it equals divine prosperity.

This is what a book can do,
its all about marketing

FILL YOUR REVENUE FUNNEL WITH A PUBLISHED BOOK
THE PERFECT PUBLISHING SYSTEM

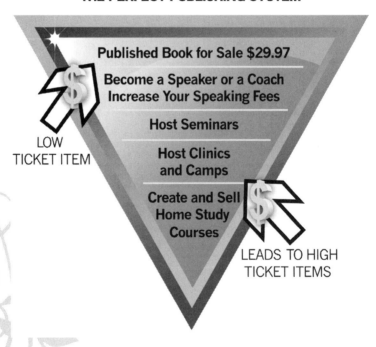

Harness the Power of Networking

IF YOU PLAN to own and operate your own business, it's crucial that you understand the importance of networking. That word may be intimidating to less socially outgoing entrepreneurs, but it is essential that you meet and interact with potential associates and customers. Not only are you going to have to grasp and embrace the concept, you're going to have to master it! Many people avoid using networking as a marketing tool because they think it is a difficult task that involves hard-pitch sales tactics and pushiness. In fact, networking is fun. It's simply taking the time to meet like-minded people, exchanging ideas with them, and offering to help each other. Some people approach networking simply as a way to promote their own advancement, but that is NOT the way to network. At the opposite end of the spectrum are the people who don't think they have anything to offer, so don't bother. We all have something to offer. Even the most inexperienced person may have an unusual trait or nugget of knowledge that the most seasoned veteran could benefit from knowing.

The goal of networking is not simply to collect contacts for your own use and to force your agenda on someone else. It should be a reciprocal process carried out with mutual respect and for mutual benefit. Networking is collaborative and everyone should benefit from it, though invariably, some will benefit more than others. What you put in, you get out. You are in possession of skills and knowledge that can help other people, and there are people out there who have something you need, want, or can use—you just haven't met them yet. When people take time out of their busy schedules to meet you, talk with you, or help you, remember that and even if you can't help them at that moment, you can give your assistance to someone else. Pay it forward. Networking is a great tool that can help you and your colleagues succeed. When you attend a meeting, conference, or even a social gathering, keep the interests of others in mind. This makes networking effortless, enjoyable, and productive. By listening to others, you gain valuable knowledge, and by paying it forward, you'll soon begin to notice that others are listening intently to you and paying attention to what you have to say!

Mentoring is a Valuable Process and an Invaluable Relationship

IN THE OLDEN days, people learned new trades by becoming apprentices. To this day, in many countries and in certain professions, one can only ascend to certain positions by spending years under the tutelage of an expert. Apprenticing is not as common today as it once was, but the theory remains as solid as ever.

I highly recommend having a mentor or two. I have three. My main mentor is Tasso Lakas as I mentioned in the earlier chapter. Their success in business and in their field can help you limit your mistakes and help you achieve your goals. Mentors can give you with powerful and straightforward advice by sharing their experiences and the lessons they've learned. Keep in mind that, just like networking, the relationship should benefit both the mentor and the mentee. It is a two-way street. The mentor benefits from the opportunity to strengthen their leadership skills, while you receive career guidance and helpful advice that will help you reach the next level of your career.

When you want to launch a new venture, always take the time to do some research. Who has succeeded in this field? Who has failed, and why? Remember, you don't have to reinvent the wheel; you simply have to create a product or service that will offer a high return on investment and a high level of customer-client benefit. In other words, a product or service that fills a gap in a particular market or industry. One incredible example of this is Facebook, a social networking site that helps us connect and share information with the people in our lives. Even though there are many competing online social media websites, Facebook has certainly won the race.

Organize Your Life

OVER THE COURSE of my career, I've had the opportunity to meet many successful individuals. They were unique, came from different backgrounds, and were superstars in different fields. Despite their differences, they all had one trait in common—they were organized. Before I understood the power of organizing my life, I was always amazed by how spotless all of these executives' desks were. I wondered, "How can they have such a clean desk? Shouldn't such a busy executive's desk be piled high with work?" Now I understand that one of their secrets to success was organization.

When we're unorganized, our lives are filled with clutter that weighs us down. Things continually need to be stored, cleaned, insured, and sometimes used as a stepping stool for an extra boost to reach the top shelf of your closet. Organization is an ongoing process that must become automatic.

Clutter costs you valuable time, and what is time? Money! Clutter doesn't only consist of clothes and paper—it can also be made up of people, organizations, and activities. Everything in your life that no longer has a specific and useful purpose should be considered clutter. Thinking of people as dispensable clutter may sound a bit harsh, but we all outgrow certain people eventually. I don't know why we feel the need to hold on to people who drag us down or never seem genuinely happy for our accomplishments, but we do. Ridding ourselves of people who don't contribute positively to our lives doesn't have to be harsh, abrupt, or cruel. If you truly want to succeed, you must eliminate unnecessary emotional, physical, mental, and financial drains on your strength, time, and well-being. If someone in your life is an energy sponge, cut them loose so they can find other friends who they are more compatible with. You have better things to do!

How many wasted minutes do you spend every day searching for your keys, cell phone, file folder, or anything else you need? The average person loses an hour a day searching for misplaced items. That's astonishing! How much profit could you have generated in that one hour? One of the first time savers is to go through all of your excess papers, shredding what you don't need and filing what you must keep. Be brutal, at your home and your office. There is no need to keep old newspapers, magazines, or catalogs, so just let go.

Take ten minutes every evening, or first thing every morning, to plan and prioritize your day by making a list of what you'd like to accomplish. When you're focused on what you need to do, you can avoid starting too many projects and not finishing any of them. Also, how great does it feel to draw a line through a completed task? Fantastic!

How much clutter do you have on your desk? How many papers and pictures are up on the walls around you? Are you surrounded by stacks of paper? All of these things distract you from your task at hand. As these distractions grow, so does your level of stress. A clutter-free, distraction-free, stress-free workspace is much more productive. Keep only a few personal items on your desk and in the surrounding work area. Think about all the stuff in your office. How much of it really needs to be there? If you answer that question honestly, you'll probably realize that most of it can go. We tape funny cartoons on our door to make us laugh and keep old nametags from a conference we went to three years ago, but all of these items are just unnecessary distractions. The only item I recommend posting on your wall or door is an inspirational quote or a list of goals.

If you have piles and piles of paper stacked in your office, make an appointment with yourself to gather these all into one pile, and process them one at a time. This is the last time you are going to handle these papers. Most of them can be thrown away or shredded, and the important ones should be filed away neatly where they can easily be found. I know most people don't enjoy filing paperwork, but don't procrastinate and let it pile up. There is no point in keeping something if you can't put your hands on it when you need it, so devise a system that works for you, and file papers as soon as you get them.

Decluttering your computer and desktop is just as important as decluttering your office. Delete the unused icons off your desktop and limit the amount of folders you have stored on your computer. Transfer any old material to a USB drive or delete it. I used to open my e-mail and see over 1,500 messages. Just looking at my inbox made me feel anxious. I've learned to delete the messages I don't need and archive the rest, so they're not distracting me each time I open my inbox. Go through your desk drawers and filing cabinets one at a time, tossing junk and only keeping what's needed. Allocate a place for everything, and make sure you always put things back in their place. This will have a tremendous freeing effect on your psyche and will open up channels of thought that were blocked by clutter.

Learn to say no. Prioritize your life by making certain you have time and energy for all the things that are important to you. The best way to do that is simply by saying no to things that don't fit into your priority scheme. Let's face it, you can't be everywhere and do everything. If you try, you'll be miserable, those around you will be miserable, and you will end up accomplishing nothing. Multi-tasking is nothing more than fracturing. Instead of picking up a whole mirror, you're shattering it and picking up the pieces one at a time. Are you accomplishing more? No, you're just busier. Instead of devoting an hour of your time to your child, you'll spend fifteen minutes doing laundry, fifteen minutes answering e-mails, fifteen minutes reading your child a story, and fifteen minutes talking on your cell phone. Have you accomplished more? The laundry isn't finished, your child is unsatisfied, there are still more e-mails to read, and you need to call your friend back. Focus is more important than a scatter-shot approach.

One recent expert said that people consider talking on their cell phone while driving multi-tasking. In fact, the mind can only focus on one thing at a time, so they are actually only giving half their attention to driving, and half their attention to the conversation. Neither task is getting the benefit of full attention; therefore, both tasks are being shortchanged.

One very important place that most people neglect to organize is their mind. Today more than ever, we are stressed, overworked, and overwhelmed. But how do you declutter your mind? You can't physically remove items from your mind like you can from your home and office. You can, however, clear your mind with the following simple actions:

- **Meditation:** Take a few deep breaths, and just focus on your breathing for a few minutes. Concentrate as the air comes into your body, and then as it goes out. This has a calming effect, especially if you continue to return your focus to your breath whenever your mind strays. Set time aside for quiet meditation every day.

- **Journaling:** If you have a lot on your mind, write your thoughts down in a journal. This process takes them out of your mind puts them onto the paper, and the act of writing can often clarify thoughts.

- **Eliminating:** What things in your life are not truly important to you? What are you thinking about right now that isn't on your short list? By eliminating as many of these things as possible, you can clear your mind and gain clarity of purpose.

- **Resting:** Lack of sleep causes your mind to race uncontrollably and makes you feel exhausted. Use the meditation technique to relax your body and mind, and sleep will soon follow. (Sleep specialists recommend a cool dark room free of electronic distractions.)

- **Exercising:** Exercising is a great way to rid your mind of the worries of the day. I recommend cardio or weight training daily, even if it is only 30 minutes, it's better than nothing. I rise at 5:30 to do my work out so there is no excuse.

- **Releasing:** Negative emotions like worry, anger, frustration, and jealousy merely fill your mind with irrational and unproductive thoughts. Let them go. This is easier said than done, but once you learn to master this technique, you will feel much better.

Organizing and prioritizing the things in your life is a significant step toward wealth, happiness, and freedom. As your outer world influences your inner world, your life becomes balanced.

Look toward Distant Horizons

I SET NEW goals every day. It is important to challenge yourself because that is how you grow, mature, and expand your mind. While long-term goals remain fixed, short-term goals should be flexible and renewable. As you achieve short-term goals, replace them with fresh ideas. Constantly challenge yourself by moving the goalpost.

Never in history has knowledge been more accessible than it is today. We are blessed with fantastic libraries, inviting and relaxing retail bookstores, and of course, the Internet, where knowledge is always just a click or two away.

It is also important to nurture your mind with uplifting information from books and wise people. Though it may seem counterintuitive, try to limit your exposure to the news. News stories are predominantly negative, and don't nurture the development of a beautiful mind or of logical mental faculties. After all, the news is designed to tell us all the horrible things going on in the world, from accidents and natural disasters to crime and corruption. While we do need to keep abreast of certain news items for our own safety and business acumen, small doses are the best medicine.

As I've already mentioned, goal setting is vital for achieving success in any endeavor. Every great success can be attributed to the creation of a clear and specific goal, and a plan for reaching that goal. Success is rarely, if ever, an accident. Because we've all heard about goal setting so often, we tend to ignore it because we think we know everything there is to know about it. Unless you practice setting goals daily, you're not taking advantage of its benefits.

The goals we set create our destiny. The surest way to achieve success in your career or business is to pick something you love and then do it well. In other words, focus. To reach your goals you must have peace of mind, a reliable income structure, and a clutter-free environment. If your chosen endeavor is a solitary one, have a support or solid infrastructure in place such as friends, family, or mentors to advise you since you can certainly work alone and launch a company alone. Then hire independent contractors so you can focus on what you're good at and leave the rest, such as bookkeeping and design, to others. It is important that you employ or contract talented, honest, and dependable people and then treat them with gratitude and respect. Remember that independent contractors and freelancers work for many other employers, and their referrals can often become sources of revenue for your business.

We all have goals, whether we know it or not. Unfortunately, many people have bad goals, goals by default, or only very short-term goals with no long-term objectives. Bad goals, which are negative in nature or unrealistic, create an unfulfilled life. Realize that no matter what your goals are, they affect your life every single day. We need goals that inspire us and encourage us to achieve greatness and be positive influences in the lives of others. Strong and compelling goals drive us toward the vision we have for ourselves and our lives. Set goals that challenge your present abilities and position in life, but that are attainable.

Without goals, you are stumbling aimlessly from task to task with no clear pathway to success. People without goals tend to meander through life, drifting from one job or project to another without ever accomplishing anything tangible. We must set goals for every area of our lives so that we continuously grow emotionally, spiritually, physically, financially, and in our relationships and our attitudes. The moment you set goals, things start changing because your expectations of yourself and your life have become clear. You are acknowledging, to both your conscious and unconscious mind, that you are not satisfied with your current state and you want to move forward.

We need to realize that at the end of our lives, it is not the money we've earned, the car we drive, or the house we live in that will matter. What will matter is who we became as a person. Strive to set goals that align with your ultimate life purpose. When it comes to setting goals, know that purpose is stronger than outcome. Purpose gives you a reason to attain something, and a reason motivates you to take action.

Goals direct our focus, and without focus our vision is blurry and vague. Success is the progressive realization of a worthy goal or ideal, and a fuzzy vision will not lead to success. Don't let fear of the time it will take to accomplish something stand in your way. The time will pass anyway, so we might just as well put that time to the best possible use. In five, ten, or twenty years you will either be right where you are today, or you will be sitting atop the pinnacle of success. The choice is yours. Your destiny is in your hands.

Success is not only measured in terms of professional achievement. Mothers or fathers who care for their children and raise them with all the proper tools for life are definitely successes. Someone who devotes their life to helping others but doesn't earn big bucks is definitely a success. Goals should focus on what we desire most for our lives and ourselves. Write down your own definition of success, and when you achieve it, you will know without doubt the meaning of the word.

Believe in your goals, regardless of previous "failures." Start afresh, forget the past, and do it properly. Renew your focus by organizing your life, decluttering your mind, and tackling your goals from a place of faith. Believe in yourself and watch your life soar to great heights of happiness and fulfillment. Above all, enjoy life! It is a gift of immeasurable value, so live it with passion. Everything you dream of and envision for yourself is out there, waiting for you. The only thing you need to do is to go and get it, and realize that the first step is to set a goal strong enough to pull you there.

To be truly successful, you must find your purpose and pursue it with 100 percent of your passion and enthusiasm. If it is truly your purpose, the money and life's rewards will follow. At the beginning of this chapter, I included my favorite quote: you reap what you sow. This is not only a biblical quote, it is also an immutable universal law—The Law of Compensation. If you experience a temporary setback, don't be discouraged. Understand that buried within your problems are hidden blessings waiting to be discovered. Like nuggets of gold buried under coal, or hidden treasure beneath a roiling sea, when you are beaten down by adversity, find solace in the Law of Compensation and look forward to the benefits that await you.

There are many goals I have yet to achieve in my journey through life. I want to make a difference in others' lives and make a positive contribution to the world. We are nothing if we can't take a moment and help our fellow sisters or brothers. Every step I take is a stepping-stone toward creating a better world. I wouldn't change one moment of my life so far, because every single one, whether good or bad, has made me the person I am today. I have had such an exciting journey so far, and I am certain that the best is yet to come.

Take the first step on your path—even if it's a baby step—and soon you will be striding confidently toward your dreams!

Felicia Pizzonia
Babe in Chocolate

About Felicia Pizzonia

FELICIA PIZZONIA has spent more than a decade cultivating her national and international marketing expertise. Felicia has assisted more than 100 authors in completing and marketing their books on the international level. A partner in Ultimate Publishing House, Felicia now combines all of her experience to produce quality books for entrepreneurial authors. Her first book, Babes in Business Suits: Success Secrets of the Top Women Entrepreneurs of the World (2009), is a testament to her desire to help all business people succeed and grow their business. Her second book is scheduled to be released in the Spring of 2010, titled *Babes in Business Suits, Dynamic Duos Share Success Secrets.* She sits as an executive director on a Canadian Federal Non Profit Organization called G.E.L. Healthier Youth Campaign, www.geltogether.org, dedicated to motivating youth and teens onto healthy habits and exercise.

COMPANY NAME: Ultimate Publishing House

WEBSITES: www.babesinbizsuits.com
www.ultimatepublishinghouse.com

EMAIL: Felicia@FeliciaPizzonia.com

BONUS GIFT:
FREE 60 minute, book manuscript review!
Plus a free guide to how to publish an E -book in 90 days
including a FREE website domain consultation!

Onward and Upward

ONWARD AND UPWARD

When Destiny calls the first time,
PICK UP THE PHONE! Every
successive call thereafter incurs
unknown charges.

— **Donna Trimboli**

"I've never sought success in
order to get fame and money:
it's the talent and the passion
that count in success."

— **Ingrid Bergman**

Women are emerging into the forefront of society, changing the traditional views of their personal and professional lives. As we evolve into our newly defined roles, we realize just how much we're capable of achieving and the significant impact we can make on the world. *Babes in Business Suits* demonstrates the levels to which women ascend. Each Babe has overcome various struggles and challenges, including difficult childhoods and financial, emotional, and physical challenges. We all have a place in business, whether as the owner of a home-based business, as the CEO of a Fortune 500 company, or in a joint venture with a spouse or life partner. As your own personal awareness of your value grows, leave no stone unturned along your path to freedom.

Knowing your purpose in life and living it to the fullest is the key to empowerment. Use these women's stories as encouragement to help you take the next step toward the life you deserve. Realize that it's okay to experience fear, lack of confidence, and low self-esteem from time to time. In fact, you're in good company, because each Babe, at one time or another, was in your shoes. With a strong belief in yourself and a driving passion, you can accomplish any goals you set, just like they did. Remember that it is okay to ask for help every now and then. Many of these ladies made it to the top with the help of others, and they want to show you the same kindness by offering you their knowledge, expertise, and inspirational life story.

More and more women are realizing that they can own and operate a business as well as raise a family. As you read each of these phenomenal ladies' stories, I hope you see that success isn't slotted for just a few. You, too, can reap the benefits of entrepreneurship and contribute to the world. My goal is that *Babes in Business Suits* will help you realize your dreams.

If you are ready to venture into the corporate or entrepreneurial arena, learn from these women and ask yourself what you want to create in your life. You have to take action and follow your desire—don't just wait for things to happen. And remember, don't try to reinvent the wheel. Many women have gone before you, so take their advice and learn from their mistakes. Whenever you get discouraged, remind yourself of the way the *Babes in Business Suits* turned obstacles into opportunities. Look at yourself in the mirror every day and ask, "How can I be my best today?" Be open to new ideas and don't be afraid to step out of your comfort zone.

In business, it is imperative to set an example by acting with integrity, ethics, and sincerity—a profit isn't a profit if it's at the expense of others. If you are already in the business of your dreams, I hope that you are enjoying success and becoming all you can be. If not, I hope that *Babes in Business Suits* inspires you and gives you the confidence to move forward in the direction of your desires.

Read each word with the certainty that this book will change your life. You can have it all: A family, husband, and a career. This life is the only one you will have, and the time to fulfill your dreams is now, don't live by the so-called rules, create your own otherwise you are just existing and that is really not any fun. I wish you the best in success.

Blessings, *Felicia*

PROVERBS

This section is dedicated to my grandfather, Natale Pizzonia, who is a great inspiration of integrity, love and peace and taught me since I was four years old to be a woman of peace and power. Natale Pizzonia lives in Calabria, Italy and is an infamous artisan and philosopher. ***Grazie Nonno, ti voglio bene.***

"Dimmi con chi vai, e ti dirò chi sei:
Tell me whom you go with and I shall tell you who you are.

Chi di natura nasce, negare non su può:
He who is born a certain way, cannot deny it.
A variant of the proverb that assures that in matters of human nature there is rarely or never any change.

Lunga a corda o curta la cudera l'omu comu nasci è sempre di na manera:
Whatever a man is born, he remains], that is,
"people are helpless to change their predetermined fate"

Chi di speranza vive, disperato muore:
He who lives off hopes dies in desperation.
A plea to face up to the realities of life; not live on hopes because hopes are usually fleeting and insubstantial.

Chi nasce quadro, non muore tondo:
[He who is born square does not die round].
i.e., some things never change.

Chi non si misura è misurato:
"He who does not measure himself is measured."

Chi misura se stesso, misura tutto il mondo,"
[He who measures himself measures the whole world].
All these proverbs imply a sense of system of justice in life, whence the
English, "what goes around, comes around."

Chi si confida i suoi segreti è scacciato dal mio regno:
[He who reveals his secrets is driven from my kingdom].
Secrets are not to be revealed.

Chi tardi arriva, male alloggia:
[He who arrives late gets badly lodged].
A variant of "The early bird catches the worm."

Chi troppo vuole, niente ha:
[He who wants too much, gets nothing].
One must regulate one's wants and be moderate in his/her wishes for
fear of getting nothing.

"Chi troppo abbraccia, nulla stringe,"
or "chi piú abbraccia, meno stringe."

[He who embraces too much, presses nothing; he who embraces more,
presses less]. A chiasmus based on "abbraccia" and "stringe."
Urges some moderation in a quest: more applicable to wishes
in the metaphorical sense.

"De fegure tristi bisogna reguardarsi"
[Beware of sad figures].

Chi va piano va sano e va lontano:
[He who goes slowly goes healthily and far].

Contro la forza la ragione non vale:
[Reason is worthless against force (power)].
Quite literal meaning and needs no metaphorical nuances.

E meglio ubbidire che santificare:
[It is better to obey than to sanctify].

La pecora ti fai, il lupo ti mangia:
[You act like a sheep and the wolf will eat you].
*The proverb is built on the predatory nature of the wolf, especially
with sheep. Obviously of rustic and agricultural nature, the proverb is
a cautionary statement warning that if you are weak or seem weak,
you will be destroyed.*

Lontano dagli occhi, lontano dal cuore:
""Far from the eyes, far from the heart."
A variant of "out of sight out of mind."

Meglio poco a godere che assai a tribolare:
[It is better to enjoy a little than have a lot to worry about].
Here there is a trade-off, "poco versus assai." See Speroni/Merbury:

"Chi altri tribola, se non posa"
[He who gives trouble to others, should not rest]

Paese che vai, usanza che trovi:
[Country that you visit, mores that you find].
*A variant of "When in Rome, do as the
Romans do."*

Quando il piccolo parla, il grande ha gia parlato:
[When the child speaks, the elder has already spoken].
*i.e, the education that the young receive is a reflection of the elder's;
also would deal with manners.*

Babes in Business Suits™

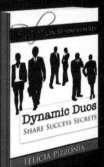

The publishing world has changed dramatically. In the new economy with global opportunities, you are either distinct or extinct, the choice is yours.

A book is the ultimate branding tool that offers:

- Credibility
- Visibility
- Distinction
- Positions you as the Expert in your field
- Media Exposure
- Attract more clients or patients
- Opportunities for product endorsements
- Its time you publish your own book with the Ultimate Publishing House!

Call today to start your book, it is the best marketing investment you will ever make!
647 883 1758 OR
Email: Felicia@FeliciaPizzonia.com

To order your copy of *the* **2010 CALENDAR**
of the **TOP 12 BABES** *featured in the book*
Email: *babe@babesinbizsuits.com*

Jeri Walz

Babe in Tweed

Dr. Cynthia Barnett

Babe in Red

Di Worrall

Babe in Ivory

Lene Hansson

Babe in Purple

Marianne Ford

Babe in Black

Mona Jagga

Babe in Orange

Sherry Wilsher

Babe in Pink

Karen Lauderback

Babe in Green

Clarissa (Riza) Gatdula-Calingasan

Babe in White

Joanne Hill

Babe in Blu

Sally Walker

Babe in Pinstripe

Felicia Pizzonia

Babe in Chocolate